ULTIMATE EDITION

Acknowledgments

Edited by Lea Galanter

Cover Design by Mars Dorian

First Printing, 2016

Advance Praise for the Series

"Due to my tenure in the games business, people often ask me how they or their kids can get a start in the video game trade. I invariably direct them to the Video Game Careers series of books as an excellent place to start. Hardy LeBel paints a straightforward and useful picture of the industry that serves as a good launching point for students and aspiring game makers."

- Zack Norman

Chief Creative Officer GOGII/textPlus

"Hardy LeBel's Video Game Careers series is just what an aspiring game creator needs to hear. When 'Hardy Says', you had best listen!"

- Scott Rogers

Author of *Level Up, The Guide to Great Video Game Design*

This book is dedicated to my wife Tracy, and my kids Sophia, Gilbert and Ava. Without all of you I'm nothing.

Who Should Read This Book

This book is for you if you love video games. In fact, you play them so much it scares people a little. Maybe it seems like you're obsessed. You're considering a career and you don't want to be a flight attendant, a lawyer, or a cowpuncher—you want to make video games.

This book is also for you if you know someone just like the person described above.

Video games are definitely not just for kids anymore. Hundreds of thousands of people around the world earn their livelihood making video games. Game development can be a vibrant career with exciting opportunities in a variety of interesting fields.

> ***Hardy Says****: Those already in game development could also benefit from this book if they were looking for an additional perspective on the job, tips gleaned from decades of experience in the trenches, or possibly just some more fun anecdotes to share at parties.*

What This Book Is

Video Game Careers is a series of handbooks for anyone interested in a career in video game development.

This book collects all three books of the VGC Series into one volume. It will take you through the complete journey, from a basic understanding of the games business, all the way through the hiring process, including descriptions of specific career paths, complete with professional tips and insights. Along the way, I'll offer some anecdotes from my own career to illustrate the points I'm making.

I may also occasionally try to be funny. Sorry, I can't help myself.

What This Book Is Not

This is not a how-to book on making your own games. There are lots of other resources out there for that. But along the way, I will offer tips and insights about making games gleaned from my own career—lessons that have helped me, and I know will help you as well.

Who The Heck Am I?

I've been a creative professional in the video game industry for over 20 years. You might know my design work on games such as Halo, Halo 2, SOCOM 3, Midnight Star, or Far Cry 2. You might have played some of the games I helped publish, like Dungeon Siege 2 or Jade Empire. Maybe you're even old enough to remember Oni, Pac-Man World 20th Anniversary, Vigilante 8, or the first game I ever worked on: Apocalypse (starring Bruce Willis).

One Caveat

Games are always changing. The industry continues to evolve, just as technology continues to evolve, so trends and opportunities that are hot today may change tomorrow. I will update this book to stay current, but be sure and do your own research as well.

4

Table of Contents

Who Should Read This Book 1

✧ Making a Game Maker 7

✧ Getting Trained...17

✧ Are You Ready? 25

✽ A Little About the Business......................31

✽ How the Game Industry Works 39

✽ How Games Are Made...............................45

✽ The Development Process...........................53

✽ Prototype and Planning 59

✽ Production and Beyond..............................69

✽ Collaboration 101 73

✿ Game Development Roles 79

✿ Roles in Production...................................81

✿ Roles in Game Design 93

✿ Roles in Programming 107

✿ Roles in Art 115

✿ Make Your Own Break 129

✿ Landing the Job..151

✿ The Path to Leadership 159

6

VIDEO GAME CAREERS

BEGINNER'S GUIDE

✧ Making a Game Maker

Video games are fun and cool, but making games is not at all like playing them. Often players are attracted to the industry, but find the work so different to what they had expected that they quickly burn out and move on to other fields. This chapter will help you discover whether you'd like the kind of work that you might end up doing if you get a job in the game development industry.

Find A Game You Love (With Tools)

Make a list of the games you're playing right now. Any type of game counts: mobile, PC, console—whatever you like to play.

Next, figure out if any of those games have built-in editing tools that will let you make your own content for the game. If you're not sure, take a look at the box, or the descriptions of the product online. Check the main menu of the game—that's usually where you'll find the option to make your own content.

> **Hardy Says**: *Software toys like Minecraft do not have the kind of level editing tools that you are looking for. Be sure to find a game with a built-in level editor so that you can produce levels for other people to play.*

If none of the games you're playing now have editing tools built into them, then you'll need to get familiar with a game that does. The following list of games have excellent tools that you can play with, but if none of these games appeal to you, then feel free to find a game you prefer.

- Geometry Dash: You can download this game on iOS mobile devices or through the Steam service for PCs.

- Crush the Castle 2, Bubble Tanks 3: These games (and many more) are available to play on your PC or Mac through online game aggregators like Armor Games or Kongregate.

- Far Cry 3, Halo 4, Little Big Planet 2: You can find these games for your favorite home console gaming system at your favorite games retailer.

Play The Game

Once you've got your hands on the game, you'll need to play it enough to get familiar with it. As you play, take notes and answer the following questions:

- What do you immediately notice as you play?

- What makes this game fun for you?

- If you took away anything away, would it still be fun?

- Is the game play always the same, or does it change? How often?

- What would you change about the game, if you could?

Now crack open the content editing tools and get ready for your first assignment in game development.

Your First Game Development Job

Now we're going to put your skills to the test. I want you to make some content using the editing tools that the game provided for you, and then put it out into the world so other players can try it out. That's it. No more, no less. For example, you could make any of the following things:

- A single-player level in Geometry Dash

- A themed platform-jumping level in Little Big Planet 2

- A multiplayer space in Far Cry 3 or Halo 4

- An interesting enemy tank encounter in Bubble Tanks 3

Before you go ahead and give it a try, check the next page for a resource that can help!

BEGINNER'S GUIDE

CHECKLIST

Are you tackling the first exercise in the book? The Beginner's Guide Checklist is a free guide, created to help first-time game-makers make sense of their first project, and achieve success. Get your copy at:

videogamecareerbook.com/checklist

A Few Predictions

All finished? Good. I have a few predictions about how it went for you, and we can learn a lot from your reactions.

Prediction 1: Most of you found making content for a game quite a bit harder than you imagined it would be.

Prediction 2: Most of you didn't actually put the content that you made out into the world so other players could play it.

Prediction 3: A few of you want to keep working on the content that you made. Maybe you want to improve it, or perhaps you want to scrap it and start over because you now have a better idea of how to approach the process.

If Prediction 1 Applies to You

If you found the process a lot harder than you thought it would be, that's normal. Developing games takes time and a lot of hard work. Making something all by yourself, with nobody to help you or encourage you is difficult.

Now let's do a quick mental exercise. However far you got in the process, imagine how much further you would need to go to finish something that was ready to put out into the world. That will give you an idea of how much work goes into developing a commercial product.

If Prediction 2 Applies to You

If you didn't put something out for the world to see, don't be discouraged. Creating content and showing it to other people can be intimidating. Developing that confidence takes time, but it can be learned.

If you did put your work out into the world, let me ask two follow-up questions (and be honest with yourself). Did you try your hardest, or did you just slap things together to get something done? How good is the content that you made compared to stuff that you played in the game?

> ***Hardy Says***: *A hobbyist can make anything they want and it doesn't matter. But if a pro releases bad content, the entire world will let them know about it. Poor player reactions lead to bad reviews, poor sales, and eventually the developer goes out of business.*

If Prediction 3 Applies to You

Congratulations, you probably already have the right mentality to be a game developer.

But if you're not one of those lucky few, don't fret. There are a lot of successful people in the games industry who weren't gifted with a natural talent for the work. And they've still gone far, because it's a job, not a hobby. Anyone with enough technical proficiency can learn the skills, which can be mastered by anyone with determination. You'll have to decide for yourself if you have that drive to pursue those goals.

If You Hated Every Minute of It

I have some good news and some bad news. The bad news is that, unless you can somehow learn to love it, working as a game developer probably isn't the career for you. You could still work in the games industry, but you're probably better suited doing something that's not focused on making content. The good news is that you didn't have to waste years of your life to find that out.

✧ Getting Trained

It is an open secret of the game development industry that an advanced degree in computer science (or the equivalent) is not the only way to prepare for a career making games. I'm amazed at the number people I've worked with who didn't have any kind of formal degree. They just started with a passion for games and began learning all they could on their own.

> **Hardy Says**: *I know so many talented, successful and famous game developers who got their start this way. These are folks who regularly make million-dollar (or more) projects, and you can too.*

So let's discuss what you can do to get the skills that you need before you decide whether a full education in software development is the right path for you.

Start Right Away

The ability to program computers is projected to be the number one skill employers will be looking for in the future. Not just in game development, but in virtually every field.

The great news is that there are some amazing tools to help kids learn more about programming and software development in general. In fact there is a great organization called Hour of Code that is dedicated to teaching kids about software development. Their website is a great place to start your own education.

Let's start with some of my favorite basic tools. The following tools are geared toward elementary and middle school kids, but anyone who'd like to understand basic programming concepts could start here.

- Hopscotch: A nifty app for iOS devices that teaches the basics of programming. It has a super-clear interface, charming graphics, and step-by-step instructions in a long series of ramped tutorials that walk anyone through the basics of programming. Any kid who can read and play mobile games can start learning to program here.

- Scratch: A web-based platform that allows people to program their own games, animations, and stories, and then share them with a large online community. It has links to MIT Media Lab, and is specially targeted at educators who are teaching kids about software development and programming.

• GameMaker Studio: A software platform and application that you can download to your PC or Mac. It's built around a drag-and-drop graphical interface with advanced scripting options for folks who really know what they're doing. The basic version is free to download and use, while more advanced versions and features cost money.

Once Upon a Time – At Summer Camp

I once worked with a game designer who got his start in game development at a summer camp for kids. His parents sent him away for two weeks of fun in the sun, but he stumbled across a small team of campers working on a game project and spent the time indoors with them instead. When the camp ended, the designer continued to pursue game development, learning and developing every skill he could. Eventually one of his student projects was submitted to an independent game development contest and he won a scholarship to a prestigious university.

Even at the entry level, companies are looking for people that are self-starters, and who have a passion for the work they do. Take advantage of every chance for learning and growth that comes your way – that's the best preparation you could have for any career you choose.

High (Powered) School

The amazing thing about modern game development is that many of the top-tier companies have realized that giving students access to their software engines and tools is a terrific way to get them ready for jobs in the future. The following engines are the same tools that major game studios use to make AAA titles every day. But for students, they're free for the asking!

> ***Hardy Says:*** *You'll need a powerful computer with good 3-D acceleration to run these game development tools.*

- Epic Games: Any serious gamer knows the name Unreal. It's one of the most popular and successful game franchises in history. But Epic Games, the company that makes Unreal, also licenses their game technology to anyone looking for a head start on core technology and tools. Their Unreal Engine 4 is free for academic use. Not only are their technology and tools top-notch, Epic also offers a number of fantastic tutorial videos on the web that can help anyone get started using Unreal.

- Unity: Not to be outdone, Epic's number-one competitor, Unity, offers an amazing game engine and tools free to anyone to download. Like Epic, Unity offers a full range of tutorial videos to help you learn and master their tools. One highly attractive feature of the Unity engine is that you can effortlessly port your game work on to other hardware platforms. This makes it the ideal choice for projects with a limited budget, but with aspirations of reaching the widest possible audience across multiple hardware types.

- Source: Finally, you could dig into the popular Source engine from Valve. The Source engine is the basis for a majority of the most popular competitive online games on the market today, from the worldwide phenomenon that is Counter-Strike to the hat-wearing madness of Team Fortress 2. If you're serious about building an online competitive game, Source is the place to start.

Many high schools have developed specialty classes and student organizations dedicated to game development. Look for classes, clubs or organizations that are focused on the practical skills and get involved.

(Even) Higher Education

Teaching yourself game development isn't the only way to go, nor is it the best option for everybody. Different people have different ways of learning, and educational programs that teach the skills to work in software development can be a good investment for aspiring game-makers. Many of the skills included in Chapter 3, "Are You Ready?," are part of the core curriculum at accredited schools. Student projects add a great deal of practical experience that helps prepare aspiring developers to be working professionals.

If you're considering attending a school of higher education to pursue training as a game developer, there are a few things to consider:

- Choose a school whose game development curriculum has a good reputation. This can have a huge impact on your career. One prominent Southern California university features a game demo day where student teams show off their work to game industry representatives. The school does an excellent job of publicizing its program, and often the visiting professionals come seeking to hire particular students for key roles.

- Pay attention to the practical side of the program: Even at highly regarded schools, some programs don't make the practical skills of game development a mandatory part of the studies. That same prominent Southern California university doesn't require students to take classes in programming, scripting, level design or computer art, and they are instead offered as optional electives. Make no mistake— game companies are looking for superstar candidates, and practical experience is the best way to prove that you can handle the challenges of a professional situation. Check to see if the program you're interested in has a format for student -directed and -driven projects. Sometimes these take the form of particular classes with playable deliverables as part of the program, or placement as an intern at a local development studio.

- Consider the "crossover" effect: Some high-profile school programs farm out game-development work to other schools. The core development work of a student-directed game might be done on campus, but art assets are often created by students at dedicated art schools elsewhere. If a high-priced program seems out of reach, perhaps find a "sister school" or an affiliate to the game-development program. This can be a great way to get in the backdoor.

If you decide that a four-year degree is the way you'd like to proceed, college assessment listings in places like The Princeton Review are a great way to weigh the strengths of the various programs.

Don't Wait - Participate

I hope you're excited by all the possibilities that are available to aspiring game developers. In addition to the tools and resources that I've listed, there are hundreds, if not thousands, more resources available on the web, including blogs, websites, forums and YouTube videos, with more appearing every day.

In addition to the tools, fantastic communities have sprung up around game development. "Indie" game development is a thriving community of game makers around the world. For one week every year they unite during the Global Game Jam, but you can find organizations year round near you through services like Meetup.

So, what are you waiting for? Get out there and get started!

✦ Are You Ready?

When people ask me what kind of education they need to get into game development. My answer is usually, "How much do you already know about it?" This chapter provides some simple exercises to help determine how much you already know, and the areas you might need to focus on before pursuing a career in games.

Your Assessment

Aspiring game developers come from a wide variety of backgrounds. It can be hard to know if you have skills that might apply. The following is one of those cool, points-based tests to figure out where you fall on the "Readiness Index." Your score will give you some insight into how well you'll be able to handle the tasks of the job, and help identify your strengths as well as areas where you could grow.

Answer each of the questions on the following page and assign points based on the following scale:

- 0 points I don't know anything about it

- 1 point I've had a little experience with it

- 2 points I usually get the results I want

- 3 points I help other people with that

- 4 points I'm a pro

> **Hardy Says**: *If you feel like you fall somewhere in between two categories, I recommend being safe and picking the lower score.*

The Questions

- How much do you know about video games?

- How good is your general computer knowledge?

- How familiar are you with computer hardware and/or networking?

- How well do you know the Microsoft Office suite of products?

- How well do you know the Adobe Creative Suite products?

- How well do you know SketchUp, or Autodesk Maya, Mudbox, or 3-Ds Max?

- Have you ever done any 2-D or 3-D animation?

- How well do you know a licensed game engine like Unreal Engine or Unity?

- How well do you know game scripting?

- Do you know any programming languages (C#, C++, HTML)?

The following questions are Yes or No. Give yourself 5 points for each Yes:

- Have you ever completed a solo software project? *

- Have you ever completed a team software project? *

 *End-of-semester or end-of-year school projects count.

Finally, for the following questions, give yourself 10 points for each Yes:

- Do you have a degree in any form of computer art?

- Do you have a degree in computer science or software engineering?

- Have you ever worked on a shipped game?*

* Test, production assistant, or audio engineer jobs count.

Readiness Index

Now total your points and compare your score to the index below:

0 to 6 points: You would benefit from more exposure to technology and development before you decide that a game career is the right path for you.

7 to 15 points: You have some technical exposure. Try exploring some new areas or taking on some project work.

16 to 25 points: You're very close to being ready. Try focusing on mastering an area that interests you.

26 to 34 points: You would be comfortable handling the kind of work common in a development environment.

35-plus points: You're ready to take on the software development world. Go get 'em tiger!

What Does It Mean?

Your Readiness Index score is meant as a tool for you to judge how much pre-development experience you've accumulated, and how much of it might be relevant to working as a professional game developer.

A score of 35 or higher does not mean that you're guaranteed to land a job at a game studio, but it does mean that, should you follow the process in Book 3 of this series - Game Jobs, and land a paying gig in game development, you'll find that you're already familiar with the types of challenges and tasks that you'll be asked to face.

Get involved in some projects, and start building your score today.

30

VIDEO GAME CAREERS

ABOUT THE INDUSTRY

❋ A Little About the Business

A lot of folks seem to have the wrong image of game development. I can't tell you how many times, after mentioning that I work in video games, someone has asked, "Oh, so you get to play games all day?"

I've given up trying to explain it. Mostly I just laugh uncomfortably and change the subject. But misconceptions like that are one of the reasons why I wrote this book. I want aspiring developers to have some sound, basic guidance at the start of their career journey.

Since we're not chatting at a backyard barbecue, here's what I used to say in response to that question:

> *"As you're building a game, you repeatedly play it to test the changes that you're making. But that's nothing like sitting down with a few friends for a marathon session of your favorite game. If you approach game development thinking you're going to end up with a job that's basically the same as your favorite hobby, you'll end up disappointed or fired. Or both."*

Then I'd usually drop my hot dog like it was a microphone and walk away like a boss.

Before moving on, let's set the record straight on some of the fundamentals:

Game development is highly technical work: Your success depends on how comfortable you are learning and working with technology. This might seem like a no-brainer, but I've met plenty of people who feel like it's enough to love games and have a "big idea."

Game development is software development: Making games is similar to other kinds of software development. The process follows predictable patterns that are driven by the product's engineering needs. You'll need to learn those patterns and be comfortable working within them.

Game development is not just a job for "kids": Professional game projects often cost tens, or even hundreds, of millions of dollars and can require years of effort. The most productive game developers are often established professionals who have been in the business for a long time. At the professional level, it's a real job, with big responsibilities and pressures, but with big benefits and paychecks as well.

Game development is highly competitive: Millions of people around the world love games, and every day more and more make the choice to try their hand at creating their own. It's a tough, competitive business, but it can also be a thrilling and satisfying career.

The Game Development Continuum

Video games are so popular that making games is not only a job, it's also a hobby. It's helpful to think about game development as a continuum that starts with kids playing with software toys like Minecraft or Disney Infinity and grows in complexity up to a full career as a paid developer of commercial games.

The Spectrum of Making Games

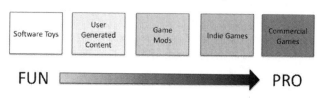

Let's take a look at the major points along that line, and the kinds of content being made.

Software Toys

Some of the most popular current entertainment titles (like the ubiquitous Minecraft) aren't even games in the strict sense of the word. Minecraft and other games like it are software toys. There is no "winning" or "losing" in Minecraft, and there's no story to follow. Players are given a confined digital world that follows specific rules, and are allowed to do anything they want within it. Disney's Infinity falls into this category, as does Microsoft's Project Spark.

User-Generated Content

Many games include built-in tools so that players can create their own content for the games that they love. In the industry, content that is made by players for other players is called user-generated content, or UGC.

Hardy Says: If you did the exercises in the Beginner's Guide, "Making a Game Maker," you made UGC.

A huge number of games support UGC, including Far Cry 3 and Halo 4, but arguably one of the most prominent games to feature UGC is Sony's Little Big Planet on PlayStation. The game, created by the development studio Media Molecule, features a powerful set of tools that players can use to make their own game content. The first levels of the game serve as a fun tutorial for all the tools you'll need to build your own worlds, and once you've completed them, a whole new universe of content opens up for you—all created by other players.

Mods

Mods (short for modifications) are extensive changes made to the art or game play of existing commercial games. Mod projects occur when fans of a game decide that, while they love their chosen game, they'd like to change a few things to better suit their own tastes. Groups of fans usually work on a mods project together. Thriving communities of modders exist who support each other and continue to build content for their favorite games for years after a game is released.

While many of these projects are done just for the pleasure of it, some mod projects have gone on to become highly successful games in their own right, such as the first-person shooter game Counter-Strike and the multiplayer online battle arena sensation Defense of the Ancients (DotA).

Mods are a terrific way for aspiring game developers to find like-minded hobbyists and dig more deeply into their favorite titles.

Independent (indie) Games

There are countless independent game developers around the world working alone or in small groups on their own game projects. But sometimes those small games become breakout hits. A few indie games you might know by name include Super Meat Boy and Don't Starve. Even the Xbox Live hit game Limbo could be considered an indie title.

Typically, indie games are not funded by major game publishers. Since they don't accept commercial funding, indie developers aren't as tightly tied to commercial success. This preserves their freedom to express their own style and values in the games they create.

Traditional indie game developers tended to operate on shoestring budgets, but the recent emergence of alternative funding models like Indiegogo and Kickstarter have given independent game developers much greater access to development funds.

Commercial Games

Commercial games are the mainstay of the game development industry. They take a wide variety of forms, from PC games that can be downloaded directly onto a home computer to cartridge-based games for handheld consoles like the Nintendo DS. Budgets for commercial games tend to range in the tens of millions of dollars, and they can employ scores, or even hundreds, of team members for years at a time.

Notable commercial game franchises include the following:

- *Call of Duty*: Developed and published by Activision

- *Assassin's Creed*: Developed and published by Ubisoft

- *Halo*: Developed and published by Microsoft

38

✷ How the Game Industry Works

In this section, I will explain just enough about the game development industry to allow you to follow along in a conversation about it, or to ask intelligent-sounding questions. But remember - a little knowledge can be a dangerous thing.

The phrase "game development industry" describes a complex ecosystem of companies that work together, and whose core business is making video games. The actual studios where games are made fall into that description, but so do the massive publishing companies, independent animation studios, contract software testing companies, advertising agencies and other related companies. If we tried to show the complexity of how these companies are connected, a diagram of the industry might start to look like the following.

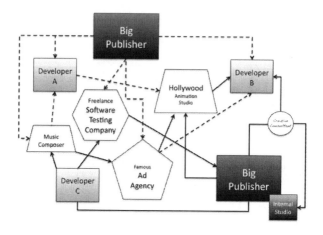

The diagram may be funny, but it also illustrates a point. The game development industry has a lot of interconnected pieces—so many that it's impossible to keep track of them all. As technology and tastes change, the industry grows and contracts to meet the evolving demands. Companies whose core business is game development must constantly evolve to keep up with the rapid pace of change, or else become irrelevant and go out of business.

So instead of trying to map the whole thing, let's just focus on the foundational business relationship: the one between publishers and developers.

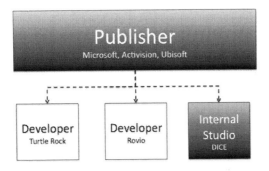

Publishers

Publishers are large companies whose core business is funding the creation of video games and bringing those games to market. They are the business people. They have all the money.

Top-tier publishing companies like Electronic Arts and Mattel, often hold the rights to high-profile licenses like NASCAR, FIFA, and Barbie. Other companies, such as Microsoft, Activision, and Ubisoft, also own major game intellectual properties (IP) outright mega-hits like Halo, Call of Duty, and Assassin's Creed.

Some publishers specialize in creating products for particular markets, but the largest companies look to leverage their IP in any way they can. They will fund development for games on every kind of gaming platform—from home game consoles and personal computers, to social media and mobile platforms.

Developers

Game development companies (developers) specialize in actually making video games. In Hollywood terms, Publishers are the money, Developers are the talent.

Developers often identify themselves as "studios," a reflection of the creative terminology used in the movie business and advertising. They range in size from small teams up to massive organizations with hundreds of people, all working on a single mega-project. Some notable development studios include the following:

- Bungie: Creators of the Halo series of games and, more recently, Destiny

- Rovio: Makers of Angry Birds

- Supercell: The geniuses behind the mega-hit games Clash of Clans and Hay Day

About Internal Development Studios

Some publishers also have internal game-development studios. Often, large publishing companies buy successful game-development studios with hit games, ensuring that the intellectual property and the team responsible for it become part of their portfolio of games. Alternately, publishers might try to create their own studios from scratch, ensuring that the company owns any hit products that come out of their work.

How Money Gets Made

Traditionally, developers come up with an idea for a game. Then they take money from Publishers to pay for the costs of building it. When the game is finished the publisher puts the game out for sale and gets their money back (and more) through selling the game. The developers usually get a royalty percentage of the sales of the game which means that it's in their best interest to try and make a hit.

The following flowchart illustrates the most common business arrangement between a publisher and a developer, and the steps involved.

The Business Steps of Game Development

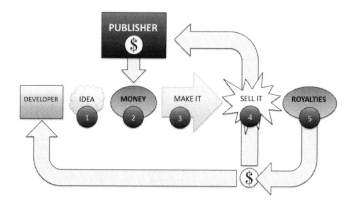

1. A developer has an idea for a game.

2. They get money from a publisher to cover their costs while developing the game.

3. They make the game.

4. The publisher brings the game to market and collects the money from selling it.

5. The developer gets royalties based on how well the game sells. (The publisher does too.)

✳ How Games Are Made

Video games are constructed using software tools on high-end personal computers. Once the pieces have been created, the development team assembles them into their final form in a process called compiling. The final form of the software runs on an underlying software engine that controls the action.

Building a Game

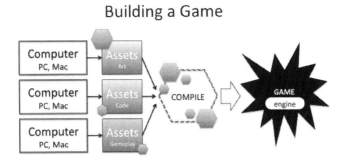

After the development process is complete, the finished game is mastered, that is, it is written onto some kind of permanent physical media and stored. The game's master copies are often used as the template for manufacturing and are carefully preserved.

Hardware Platforms

When people talk about making games, they often use the terms hardware platform or platform. These describe the various types of devices used to play games. For example, a smart phone is considered a platform. So are home gaming consoles, laptop computers or home computers.

> ***Hardy Says***: *The following diagram shows three platforms for video games, but I bet you could think of at least three more to fill in the blanks below. Stretch your brain and give it a try!*

Hardware Platforms

Computer	Console System	Mobile Device
PC, Mac	Xbox, Playstation, Wii	iOS, Android

Since we're talking about hardware, we should discuss a term that might pop up: porting. Often hit games will be ported from one platform to another, which means that they are adapted to play on other kinds of hardware. For example, a hit game in the Apple operating system might be ported to work on the competing Android operating system. Software is considered portable when the cost of adapting it to work on a new kind of machine is less than the cost of writing it from scratch.

Porting Software

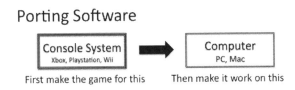

Assets

Assets are the individual pieces of a project, and include anything that appears on the screen—a character, an animation, or a sound effect. Making the game is the process of creating those pieces and then assembling them into their final, compiled form. Everything that appears on the screen is intentionally included by the developers.

Tools

Game makers use software tools on their computers to build assets for their game. Teams use common software that you might already know, like Microsoft Word, Microsoft Excel, Microsoft Powerpoint, Adobe Photoshop, and Adobe Illustrator. They also occasionally use powerful, computer-aided design (CAD) programs such as Autodesk's Maya, Mudbox, and 3-Ds Max, or Pixolobic's ZBrush to help create the in-game art.

In addition to the common suite of tools, game developers often need to create their own custom tools to help make assets for their game or to assemble their game into its final form. Many of these tools are proprietary to the companies that made them, but you can find examples of them in the various game engines available for download on the web.

Game Engines

The game engine is the complex set of programming that forms the underlying framework for a game. The engine controls the most basic systems. For example, how characters and objects move on the screen, when and how sound effects are played, how the graphics are drawn, and many other functions besides. It's those essential parts of the software that the end user (the player) doesn't actually know about or interact with.

Hardy Says: *That's where the term "engine" comes from—it's the stuff under the hood that most motorists never see, that makes the vehicle go, and that they generally don't know anything about.*

Some game developers write their own engine for their game in advanced programming languages like C++, but a few companies specialize in creating game engines and tools, and then licensing them out. These include Unreal Engine (by Epic Games), Unity (by Unity), and Source (by Valve).

Pre-made engines and tools make it possible for teams to get up and running quickly and can also be easily modified if needed. The down side is the associated cost—licensing an engine and tools to make a game that you plan to sell yourself can be an expensive proposition.

50

VIDEO GAME CAREERS

RESOURCE GUIDE

Get your FREE list of the tools, services and organizations listed in this book at:

videogamecareerbook.com/resourceguide

✳ The Development Process

I'm going to explain the steps of the development process in detail. This will help all you budding game developers wrap your heads around what the job really looks like in practice. Software development always follows the same four phases:

1.   Concept

2.   Prototype

3.   Planning

4.   Production

Each step focuses on achieving something specific for the overall development process and would be divided into a number of milestones.

Milestones

The term milestone describes a major point of achievement in a project. Teams generally use the term to help identify the achievement of a number of smaller goals within a phase of the production process, and usually across multiple disciplines. By breaking the project phases into milestones, producers can more easily manage a variety of tasks that all need to happen at the same time.

For example, a milestone might have specific goals for art, programming, and design. The tasks are tracked independently, but the team is said to have "reached" the milestone goals once all the tasks are complete.

A Request from the Author

Before I dive into describing the concept phase, let me point out that I've listened to a lot of pitches. Unless I'm sitting in a meeting held specifically for the purpose of hearing a big game idea, I generally smile and nod, and then say, "Yes, I agree. That would make a terrific game."

Unless it's a hobby project, every game project starts with a business goal. So if you're dying to make a particular game that haunts your dreams and your every waking moment, unless it's aligned with the business goals of a particular company it's unlikely to get made. Unless, of course, you find a way to fund it yourself, which is not impossible these days.

I wanted to make this point mostly so that, should we meet (and I hope we do), you don't pitch me your big idea. Please just pretend that you did, and I said, "Yes, I agree. That would make a terrific game."

Then we can stay friends.

The Concept Phase

The idea for a new product is generated during the concept phase. Once a business objective is set, the creative process can begin. Sometimes the concept for a new game will come from a particular creative person or a team:

> *"I'd like to make a game about two plumbers who eat some 'shrooms and then fall down a drain pipe into a magical world!"*

> - ***Shigeru Miyamoto*** *(possibly said this)*

> *"I'd like to make a game about small animals racing through my neighborhood. I'll call it Power Paws Racing!"*

> - ***Me*** *(I said this just now)*

Because projects are formed around business objectives, occasionally the concept for a game comes from the business department of a major game company:

> *"We just paid two squillion dollars for the rights to use images of Shaun White riding a snowboard. We need a new snowboarding title to launch during the next winter Olympic games!"*

> - ***A Marketing Lady*** *(probably said this)*

Sometimes the concept for a new product is simply the continuation of a franchise that's already successful in the marketplace:

> *"Americans like football and guns. Europeans like soccer, and also guns. Let's make another Madden football game, another Battlefield game, and another FIFA soccer game. We literally cannot lose!"*

> - ***Electronic Arts*** *(definitely said this)*

During the concept phase, the creators will sketch out the major ideas of the game. For example, I might come up with an idea and create a small pitch description that looks like this:

> **High Concept:** *Power Paws Racing is a third-person racing game featuring small animals racing through urban and suburban environments. Players can choose their own path through whimsical levels, and their animal abilities will offer special advantages, like climbing walls and trees, swimming in water, or chewing through wooden obstacles.*

Usually during this period, the creative person or team will get feedback from the folks that the company trusts the most in the creative process, the "stakeholders," who often have a great deal of say in the outcome.

Once Upon a Time - With Stakeholders

I was once invited to attend a concept retreat for stakeholders of a major franchise game owned by a large publishing company. The retreat was held in a renovated chateau isolated in the French countryside. Attending were people from both the leadership team and the development team, each an expert in a particular area of game development.

Attending from the publisher's leadership team were the chief creative officer (CCO), the gameplay specialist, the production specialist, the marketing specialist, and the project coordinator.

Attending from the development team were the game producer, the lead designer, the art director, the narrative designer, and the creative consultant.

I was struck by how deliberate the company was with their franchise. The CCO and his team had some very specific things that they, and therefore the company, needed included in the game. Some of what they said matched what the team had envisioned, but some of the directions were radically different. Once the development team was given those directions, we spent endless hours discussing the setting, characters and game mechanics.

After the retreat, the development team went back to their studio for a month to integrate the CCO's comments into their concept for the game, which would then be presented at a second meeting in front of the company's board of directors. Even the highest levels of the company had a creative stake in the process.

✳ Prototype and Planning

The prototype phase is when the team fleshes out the core ideas of the game. Many of the prototypes are intended to demonstrate that the proposed gameplay will be fun, but there can also be visual or technical prototypes to prove out concepts in those disciplines as well.

Video game prototypes can take a lot of interesting forms. Sometimes they're actually playable in a digital form, but they can also be board games or card games. I've even worked on a few projects where we stitched together video footage we found into short movies showing the approximated gameplay that the team was going for.

If I were to make a prototype for Power Paws Racing, I'd want to develop it as a board game to demonstrate how the levels might offer different animals fun, alternate paths though them. I can imagine planning out the maps with a variety of fun obstacles and secret routes for each animal. Some questions naturally arise from that process. For example, what would the skunk need its stink spray for?

In addition to the paper prototypes, I'd also want to do some digital prototyping. It would be important to ensure that the game camera and controls work well even if the animals start to climb trees or run up and down walls. And I imagine that the game would need some kind of HUD solution to allow players to keep track of each other's progress through the levels that wasn't just a traditional top-down racetrack map.

The prototype phase ends when a team has proven out enough of their core ideas so that they understand the game that they're trying to make for real.

Once Upon a Time - In Prototyping

Prototyping can be a tricky process. One of the hardest things is knowing when it should end.

Once I was overseeing an internal development team that was making a big budget on-line role-playing game. At the time, Sony's *Everquest* series was the leading title in that genre space, but the race was on for some other company to create the next big thing.

The development team had built the basics of their vision; a game that would support thousands of players on-line at the same time, with everyone pursuing quests in private adventures all over their fantasy world. It was cool, but the publisher and the team both felt that it wasn't different enough from Everquest to take the top spot, so the team dove into intensive prototyping to come up with something new.

After a year of trying various features and gameplay they hit on a cool idea, and brought everyone in to watch a demo of their idea. As we watched, a group of heroes entered an adventure space and battled their way past frost giants - the villains in Norse mythology. At the midpoint of the adventure, an army of giants marched into view, approaching from the opposite side of a bridge. There were far too many for the heroes to fight, but there was a way out. The heroes were presented with a timed challenge to destroy the stanchions holding up the bridge before the army could cross. They succeeded, and the bridge came crashing down in a dramatic animated scene, stranding the army on the far side of a huge ravine. More importantly, the wreckage opened up a new pathway, where the heroes could climb up over the rocky peaks and sneak around the army to reach their final objective.

Their innovations were the variation in the gameplay, and the cool animated sequence. It was visually spectacular, and it changed the gameplay in an interesting way. It seemed obvious that they could take this new formula and go off and make enough content to fill up their game. But there was a problem.

After the presentation I spoke to the team and they were enamored of this new technology. Instead of coming to the conclusion that their animated events were enough of an innovation, they decided that they needed to push the technology even further to create completely dynamic game spaces where just about anything could happen, based on the actions of the bad guys and the reactions of the players.

The problem was that the team had been working on their project for almost two years before they stumbled across the innovation at the heart of their product. And instead of shifting into production, they were adamant about exploring these new concepts through more open-ended prototyping.

This is one of the challenges of this early stage - you have to recognize when you've answered the major questions in your process and shift into the later phases. In the case of my example team, they refused to push the game into production and so senior executives at the publishing company cancelled their project six months later.

The Planning Phase

During the planning phase the development team comes up with time estimates of how long it will take to make the assets that will go into the game. Scores of details go into making every asset for a game, so all four disciplines participate in the planning phase. Adding anything to the list means extra work to add it to the game for real.

For example, the squirrel character in Power Paws Racing would need a 3-D model of its body, animations for the character, special gameplay code to make it different from the other animals, as well as any sound effects it makes. During the planning phase, the various teams have to do the following:

- Art team: Estimate how long it will take to create a good-looking squirrel for the game.

- Game designers: Make a plan for writing detailed design documents.

- Level designers: Estimate on how long it will take to create four fun levels to race through.

- Programmers: Estimate how long it will take to write the computer code to make the gameplay possible.

- Production team: Collect and organize all of the estimates and answers into a project schedule.

Notice that I keep talking about *estimates*. Nobody knows exactly how long a task will take unless it's been done lots of times before, and the results have been tracked. Even familiar tasks that you may have done hundreds of times before are still just estimates unless you have kept good records on how long they have historically taken.

You might disagree, saying something like, "Hardy, it takes me two minutes to brush my teeth. I've been brushing my teeth for my entire life, and I'm sure that's how long it takes." Two minutes sounds like a reasonable estimate. But unless you've been using a timer every night and have been writing the actual times down in a spreadsheet, then it's just an educated guess. What about the nights when you decide to floss? Or instances when you have a stubborn piece of popcorn shell stuck way up in-between your teeth? Or maybe you skip, because you're too tired?

Most of the tasks involved in making a new game are being done for the very first time, so the best that a team can do is estimate how long they will take. And some of those estimates will be wrong.

Let's Pretend

Imagine you and I are responsible for planning the Power Paws Racing game. To make our game, we'll need to propose solutions for each part of the project.

Engine

There are lots of things to think about when picking an engine. For example, we'll need our animals to move in a variety of ways through our racetracks. That means we'll need an engine that can handle things inside the game moving quickly (because it's a race), and in multiple dimensions (up and down walls, under fences etc.) Also, we'll probably need the game engine to be able to draw big areas to race in. After all, a tiny area doesn't make for much of an interesting race.

Our game engine will need to simulate how our racing animals move. Since we haven't yet decided if we want the movement to be realistic or cartoony and exaggerated, that will probably be an area we need to define to help pick the right kind of engine to use. Our animals will most likely bump into each other and into obstacles scattered around the tracks, so we'll need our game engine to handle collisions between objects.

Finally, let's say that our animals can be hurt if they run into dangerous hazards on the track. So our game engine needs to be able to record damage to anything caught up in collisions and possibly change the behavior and appearance of animals that are injured.

Tools

We're definitely going to need some kind of tool to lay out racetracks for the game. We'll need some way to define the main track areas, as well as parts of the course that are out of bounds. We might even want secret paths that offer special advantages. The racetrack designers are also going to need tools that will let them define the rules of the races that they are in (for example, is it a time trial? Is the winner first to three laps? Five? Do the racers start sitting still, or are they already in motion?).

We'll also need tools to define the racers themselves. For example, do all the racing animals have the same acceleration or are they different? What about how they turn or stop? If we want the animals to "feel" different as the player is controlling them, then we'll need ways to define those differences.

Assets

Finally, we'll need to make a list of all the assets that we'll need to assemble for our game. For example, we'll need the tracks, the obstacles, the animals, some way of making the hazards that appear on the tracks, the sounds of the animals, and more.

These examples should provide an understanding of some of the basic concepts in game development. Go from the imaginary to the practical. The game concept can inform you about what the engine will need to be able to do, and thinking about the assets that you'll need can help you identify the tools you'll need to make them.

One Last Comment About Schedule

I once worked with a team that was committed to creating a complete schedule for their triple-A game title. The theory was that if they could write down everything they intended to do or create and carefully assign time estimates to it, they would know precisely when the game would be finished.

But here's the thing - it took them months to try and create their comprehensive schedule - time that they weren't spending making their game. And even with all that planning, there's no way to completely account for everything that might happen in production - lucky things that happen to fall into place quickly, or unexpected problems that pop up.

I'm convinced that, if you were to write down everything you needed to do to ship a game, you'd prove beyond the shadow of a doubt that the task was in fact impossible. So when it comes to scheduling, be clear on your intentions, make reasonable estimates, and remain flexible.

✻ Production and Beyond

Once planning is complete, the process of building the game—the production phase—can get underway. Software teams have lots of different names for the stages in this phase, but basically production breaks down into three stages: alpha, beta, and post-production.

Alpha

The goal of the alpha stage is to create one working example of everything that you ultimately want to put into the game. Even if the work is rough or placeholder, the alpha stage helps the software team understand the entire scope of the project that they are building.

In our example game, Power Paws Racing, the alpha version might have one example level for players to race through, complete with one racer that players can actually play. The level would probably have rules that allow someone to win and the other players to lose, as well as examples of how animal special abilities would actually work.

In an earlier chapter, we talked about the software tools that game developers use to build their games, but this is where tools really come into focus again. If the tools don't already exist (and often they don't, especially if you're making something truly unique), then the development team must create them during the alpha phase.

For example, our Power Paws team wants to make special areas in the game maps that will allow the various racing animals to use their special abilities. But the game engine that we're using doesn't have any way to define special abilities for the animals or include them in the game. In that case, our programmers would need to add pieces to the engine to support our goals for animal abilities. For example, they might add a tool that would let our level designers mark parts of the environment as climbable by the squirrel, but not by other animals. The same tool could probably be adapted so that the designers could mark areas of water for the rat to swim in, or weak wood that the raccoon could chew through.

Beta

The beta stage is complete when everything that you wanted to put into the game is finally there. Things might not be fully polished, but everything is finally in. For that reason, beta versions of the game are sometimes called "content-complete" versions.

The beta version of Power Paws Racing would be complete when all four racing animals were working in the game, all four of the racetracks were playable with their unique features, and all of the required gameplay and other features were working as well. For example, if the game was meant to support four animals playing across the Internet, then the multiplayer parts of the game would need to be working too (networking, matchmaking).

Once a software project has reached the end of its beta stage, it can be released. But the fact is, most products that reach beta are too rough to be released to the public. These content-complete versions of the game often undergo months of polish as they are brought up to market quality.

Post-Production

Post-production is work that happens on a piece of software after it is released. It's very rare for products to go out into the market without some kind of follow-up work from the team. New bugs found by the audience need to be fixed, balance problems often need to be addressed, and new content (downloadable content, or DLC) is created to help keep interest in the game alive post-release.

Once Upon a Time - In Production

When I was working on the game SOCOM 3, the company's management team was putting massive pressure on the development team to hit its content-complete goals. Though features and tools were still incomplete, they insisted that the game hit its originally planned beta deadline.

When the deadline hit, we had a content-complete build that had some shocking flaws in it. For example, a math bug calculated the direction of bullets incorrectly, so that when a player shot an in-game gun through a transparent window, the bullets took a left turn. You literally could not hit targets on the other side of a window! The team wondered how we could possibly ship a game that was so obviously broken, and then the producers finally spilled the beans: we had an additional three months of polish time that they just didn't tell us about.

Producers can be so cruel.

✳ Collaboration 101

Game development is a collaborative art form. Just because a person has a job in one category doesn't mean that they can't have an impact on other areas of the project. For example, a producer with really good instincts about game play can still have a huge impact on how fun their project is.

> **Hardy Says**: *Remember that everybody working on a game development team has the same goal: to make a fun game. The results are much better when the process is inclusive. Just don't let the programmers try and make art.*

It's critical to cultivate the ability to collaborate. The various disciplines function best when they think of themselves as a service, helping the other departments by providing solutions from their area of expertise. No matter your discipline, it's easy to fall into the trap of imagining that your specialty is the most important part of the process.

I've worked with designers who fell back on their job title to deflect criticism, and ended up alienating their teammates. For example, here is one way a gameplay designer reacted when their design was challenged and called lame:

> "Look, I'm the game designer. It's my job to know what's fun and what's not, so this feature needs to work the way I wrote it up. End of discussion."

Don't ever act like this. The other disciplines can take the exact same stance to resist input, and the pattern quickly becomes a self-defeating cycle for the entire project. A service-oriented designer who responded as follows would probably have netted them much better results:

> "I hear that you're concerned. Let's talk about your reservations."

This approach does a few things right. First, the designer makes it clear that they are listening to their teammate's feedback. That can go a long way toward avoiding hurt feelings and bad blood.

Another example of a collaborative response from the designer receiving criticism about their design could be:

> *"The intention is for our game to occupy a space in the <x> genre. I've studied competing products, and I think my design innovates on what they've done in some exciting ways. But if you've got some technical recommendations that would make this feature better, I'd be happy to discuss them."*

The designer gently but firmly indicates that they are designing toward a specific goal, and the design has some intention behind it.

> ***Hardy Says****: If you've done your homework and you're convinced that your plans are going to move the project in the right direction, then take every opportunity you can to explain that thinking to anyone and everyone who will listen.*

The second thing that this approach does is indicate that the designer is not working in a vacuum—they've played competitive products in the genre space. Referencing other games can be a great form of shorthand because it conjures up the images and emotional impact of the finished systems in those products, not just a bunch of words and numbers on a piece of paper

Third, the designer reframes the conversation away from their teammate's subjective feelings about the system and redirects the conversation toward any potential technical concerns, which are clearly in the realm of the programmer's responsibilities.

> **Hardy Says:** *Reframing the discussion around professional responsibilities doesn't always work. But if both parties are intractable, this kind of conversation can help to establish professional boundaries. Just remember that a humble, responsive attitude builds trust and strengthens team bonds, empowering everyone to function at their best.*

Finally let me add that nobody likes being told that their work is lame. Any professional who treats other team members with disrespect when providing feedback or criticism needs to work on their communication skills.

You're Killin' Me Here...

One other challenge for anyone interested in game development to be aware of is the strong possibility of "drive-by management"—it's happened to me personally. I've worked for a long time on a feature only to have someone from senior management step in and tell me to throw out all of the work and start over.

Hardy Says: This can and will happen to anyone who is not Bill Gates.

If you're not comfortable giving up some control for the good of the group, or if you can't handle powerful people disrupting your carefully crafted plans for reasons you might not understand (or agree with) then once again, video games might not be the place for you.

78

VIDEO GAME CAREERS
GAME JOBS

❃ Game Development Roles

There are four broad categories of jobs in game development, with a bunch of subcategories. Different companies may have different names for them, but the responsibilities are pretty much the same no matter where you go.

PRODUCTION

- Executive Producer

- Producer

- Software Tester

- Quality Assurance Analyst

GAME DESIGN

- Gameplay Designer

- Level Designer

- Audio Designer

- Narrative Designer

PROGRAMMING

- Programmer

- Technical Artist

- Technical Designer

ART

- 2-D Artist

- Concept Artist

- Graphic Designer

- 3-D Artist

- Animator

The following chapters will discuss each category of jobs in detail, followed by a chapter about how these jobs work together.

❋ Roles in Production

Producers drive the schedule and keep the entire development process on track. They are often responsible for the project budget and for moving resources (people and/or computers) around to help address the various challenges that a team might encounter.

Business projects are created to achieve specific goals (usually to make money). Producers are responsible for driving the process to hit those goals, and they only succeed when they achieve the results that the company is looking for.

Imagine a company wants a cheaply made app to feature a movie tie-in toy. It's critical that the software be available for download when the associated toy is available around the world. If the assigned producer is late on delivering that app so that the software isn't available to coincide with the toy, that producer is doomed. It wouldn't matter if the game was terrific when it finally came out, or if the team that made the game was happy and healthy. In the business world, if the project fails to meet the needs of the company, it's a fail.

> **Hardy Says:** *I often hear developers lament that producers don't seem to understand the challenges of the development process. They cry that producers don't seem sympathetic to weaknesses of the flesh, or failures of the spirit. To the uninitiated, producers can seem like heartless monsters. Remember, the producers' parameters for success are sometimes at odds with the goals of the other roles. And that's not a bad thing, it's just reality.*

Also included in this discussion of production roles are testers and quality assurance analysts, those people who help ensure that the product works as designed. These entry-level, but vital, roles are often the beginning of the path toward a job in production.

Executive Producer

At the top of the game production food chain are the executive producers. They are usually the ones who decide on the business objectives at the start of every project. They command huge budgets and can deploy mighty armies of developers to achieve their objectives.

> **Hardy Says**: *Don't be deceived by their polished manners... Executive producers are ruthless predators in the ocean of business. They can haggle like a one-eyed fishmonger and schmooze like the first-born child of a politician.*

Often the executive producer "owns" a particular brand or intellectual property as a representative of the company that owns it. For example, George Lucas used to be the guy for all things Star Wars. In the case of a massive franchise like Mario, Nintendo probably has several people responsible for supervising every Mario game in development to make sure that they have the signature brand.

The Legend of Zelda: The Wind Waker is an interesting example of a product that deviated from its established brand. The art style in Wind Waker was a big change from previous games in the Zelda series, and the audience reactions were split. Part of the Zelda audience loved the new style, but there was a vocal group that rejected it entirely. I wonder if an executive producer lost their job for that choice, or if they were "too big to fail."

Producer

This job can have a lot of different names that vary from company to company, but the essence of the job is tracking tasks that come in, assigning them to one or more of the team members you are overseeing, and then tracking the progress of those tasks to make sure that they get done.

The job typically requires you to be good at tracking lots of parallel information (using software, and your own innate sense of organization) and to be dogged enough to follow up on everything you're responsible for overseeing. Since this requires interacting with people who may not have yet finished those tasks, these interactions can be tricky.

Trying to produce results from someone by pushing too hard (nagging or bullying) can alienate them, making them feel bad and quite possibly compromise your relationship with them, as well as hamper their productivity. Not pushing hard enough will lead to tasks being late or, worse, never getting finished. As discussed, those outcomes are bad for producers.

If you're a total newbie in the role of producer, you'll be a production assistant or an associate producer, working under someone more experienced as they teach you their job. Once you prove that you're capable of producing results for the company that you work for, you will most likely be a producer.

> **Hardy Says**: *Production is not a job for the shy or for the faint of heart.*

How to Progress as a Producer

Ineffective producers simply assign work to their team and expect it all to somehow get completed. The best producers learn how things really get done, and who actually does the work. Then they demonstrate that knowledge, so that team members know the producer understands the process and recognizes their contributions.

> **Hardy Says**: *Did you follow that? Figure out who the most effective people on your team are, and make sure that they know that you know. Mention their achievements in front of the team, or give them kudos in the company newsletter. Sure it sounds hokey, but people secretly love it.*

Once you've learned how your team works, make sure to shield and protect your best workers. Talented, hardworking folks are often soft-hearted, and they may be asked to work on things that are not really their responsibility. You should track that and, if necessary, intervene. Just because someone is a hard worker doesn't mean that you want them to burn out from overwork. By supported, I mean try to graciously provide some creature comforts without grumbling. Buy snacks for the team. Take them out to lunch, or buy dinner if folks are staying late to hit a deadline. Send your team members to professional conferences, or nominate them for industry awards. Those may seem like small gestures, but they can make a huge difference.

And, finally, say thank you.

> **Hardy Says**: *It's amazing how much harder someone will work for you when they understand how much you appreciate it and thank them for the effort.*

It's critical that a producer make accurate estimates on how long things will take to get done and then deliver on the predicted results. The key is to make people responsible for accurately judging their own time estimates.

Done correctly, producing will earn the grudging respect of the people that you manage. They will acknowledge (however reluctantly) that the producer constantly intervening in their natural proclivity to sit and think deep thoughts (read: surf the web) has actually enabled them to ship real software.

If you're successful as a producer, it's almost inevitable that you will find opportunities to move upward and manage larger groups on higher profile projects. That means you're on your way toward becoming an executive producer.

> **Hardy Says**: *Buy a suit.*

Tester / Quality Assurance Analyst

Software testing or quality assurance jobs are entry-level roles in the video game industry. Testers are paid to continually use a piece of software and intentionally try to "break it," finding and recording defects (known as bugs) for the development team to fix.

> **Hardy Says**: *Software testing is a hard, thankless job because, as a tester, you're always the bearer of bad news. It's also considered entry-level work because, on some level, anybody can be asked to use a piece of software.*

In the old days, when dinosaurs roamed the Earth, test and quality assurance were the same thing. But recently, companies have begun to distinguish between the tester (who tries to find defects) and the quality assurance analyst (who makes recommendations about how to improve the software).

The key to being a good tester is figuring out how to reproduce the problems you find, and documenting them carefully and thoroughly, so that when the development team finally has a minute to fix the issue, they can read your report and repair the problem with as little fuss as possible.

The other key is a certain fortitude of the soul. I'm not kidding when I say it's a hard and thankless job. Evolving in the job requires learning how not to become frustrated or bitter.

Making the shift from tester to quality assurance analyst is about building relationships with the producers and the software developers. Find a way to successfully interact with them. This may be a challenge, since they are busy and you (usually) represent bad news, but good people will make time to help mentor you. Learn as much as you possibly can about how the software that you're working on is created.

Hardy Says: Developers might not act on your suggestions, or maybe the bugs that you find won't ever get fixed—don't take that personally. Everything in software development must be prioritized. Keep finding and logging issues, learning all you can, and making connections with the developers. Once you've made some inroads, try making a suggestion or two to the people who already trust you. You will find your chance to shine.

Finally, I will add that in the most sophisticated software companies, test is actually a real career path. Sophisticated outfits (like Microsoft, for example) use things like data mining, usability labs, and psychological screening to delve into user interaction with software. It's a real career, and it's powerful stuff. If this is an area that you're interested in, I strongly advise you to work only at a company where this career path is clearly established.

Hardy Says: Don't just slave away hoping you'll get noticed—ask the person hiring you if testing is a career path at their company or not.

Once Upon a Time - In Quality Assurance

When I landed my first job in game development, I was hired on the basis of my work as a freelance writer. A very nice, soft-spoken production assistant by the name of Andy started the same week that I did. Since my background was in writing, the first two months I focused on the creative side of the project by writing cool narrative descriptions of the game world and the characters that would appear in it.

In that same time span, Andy was selflessly doing production assistant work—ordering and assembling PCs for the development team, bringing the team dinner when we all had to stay late, and following the project director around and taking care of whatever he asked. Andy was happy to do the crappy jobs around the studio, but he didn't want to remain a production assistant forever, so he continually sought out additional things he could do to help the team. One day, the programmers decided Andy could do some quality assurance work for them by helping to test and refine early versions of the level design tools they were working on before they were given to the level designers.

By the end of the first two months, I had evocative text descriptions of the game world while Andy had built a working prototype level. He was immediately hailed as a genius and moved on to the design team.

Humility. Curiosity. Hard work. Perseverance. These can take you where you want to be.

Postscript: Andy was the only person I ever worked with who, after earning his break into games, voluntarily decided to walk away. As he was leaving, I expressed my shock that he was going to another industry. He just smiled and said, "It's too much pressure. I don't need that kind of stress in my life." I have always admired how much self-awareness he showed by making that decision.

✽ Roles in Game Design

"Design is intelligence made visible."
Alina Wheeler

No, I don't know who she is either, but I have that quote tattooed across my chest, backwards, so that I can see it in the mirror every day. Perhaps the ultimate job in game development is game design—the one that drives the fans wild, and can make you famous enough to get your face on the cover of game development magazines around the world.

> ***Hardy Says****: I did not say it would make you rich and powerful. If your goal is to be rich and powerful, you should probably stick to programming or producing.*

But hey, I'm not bitter. I'm happy with the career path I chose. I'm not at all resentful of those rich and powerful programmers with their fancy cars and their rock-star lifestyles.

Honestly. I'm okay.

Most aspiring game developers love playing games. But loving games does not necessarily translate into a real understanding of how games actually work, or what makes them fun. Here's the thing to remember: every part of a user's experienced is designed. The buttons you click, the sounds your hear, even how the software makes money—everything. And carefully thinking about those choices is the job of the game designer. Everything that makes it into a game is designed by somebody.

However, when talking about design jobs in game development, we're primarily talking about two things: gameplay design and level design. These two jobs have very different responsibilities and skill sets, but both have to work closely together to make a game fun.

> *Hardy Says: Imagine if the person deciding how high Mario can jump (the gameplay designer) didn't talk to the people building the levels with things to jump over (the level designers), so that every block in the game was too high to jump over. That would not be a fun game.*

Gameplay Designer

Games are built around complex sets of data, so gameplay designers (aka data designers, aka game designers, aka systems designers) spend their days fiddling with numbers.

Let's continue using Mario as an example. It will probably come as no surprise that gameplay designers are the ones who decide things like how fast Mario can run, how a wall-jump game mechanic works, how sensitive the D-pad should be to pick up steering in mid-air, or when you have to press the controller buttons to make Mario do a butt-slam attack. But they don't just do it for Mario. They're also involved in designing all the enemies that Mario might run into during the game. And they have to set up all the data for the bad guys as well—how fast they move, how high they jump, and if they have special rules about how to defeat them.

Designing the data for a game is a huge job, and it's critically important because, as we all know, if the game doesn't feel right when you're playing it, the game isn't fun.

I could tell you a lot of stories about designers who wrestled with gameplay balance and failed to make their games more fun. But sharing those stories would be a cruel and counterproductive. After all, those designers wanted to make games that were fun and beloved by one and all, but they failed. One tip I can offer that can help gameplay designers push their titles to where they need to be in terms of fun: Let the game speak to you.

How to Progress as a Gameplay Designer

Gameplay design is hard. We've all played games that weren't fun, and behind most of those games were experienced designers who were tackling the challenges of gameplay design and struggling. I happen to believe that some people just have a knack for it—a talent for making the numbers and systems work. But there are some things you can do to help put you on the path toward fun. I talk about these techniques at length on my blog; see if it helps. If not, contact me and I'll help you fix it.

If you do a good job making stuff fun, you will earn the trust of your coworkers and you will likely be given more opportunities to create and balance gameplay systems. That's the path to becoming a lead designer of perhaps even creative director.

> **Hardy Says**: *Start wearing a lot of black.*

Level Designer

People often ask me about the best level design I've ever seen, and my answer is a little odd. Before I got started in the game business, I lived in New York City, and I would visit Central Park. I can distinctly recall walking through open air spaces that gave me a feeling of physical refreshment, or finding interesting cloistered switchbacks that led to little ponds or hidden fountains—social areas that created a sense of wonder and exploration in me. I remember thinking, "Wow, this place is just what I needed. It's so nice to have some nature in the middle of the city."

Years later I learned that every square foot of Central Park was designed to create those feelings in visitors. The landscape of the park was the work of the genius landscape architect Frederick Law Olmsted, and the spaces were carefully and thoughtfully composed. To me, that's level design at its highest. It is creating spaces that evoke particular emotional responses from the user. They might be calm and restorative feelings (like walking through Central Park), or they might be claustrophobic and terror-inducing (like running for your life through the sewer tunnels in Half-Life 2). The best levels tell a story, and they do so in an artful and unobtrusive way.

But level design is much more than just telling a story. As I said before, level design and gameplay design have to work hand in hand. Every game needs its levels to be built to take full advantage of the gameplay design. Even a first-person shooter needs levels built around the way the player is able to move and the way the weapons work in the game. For example, the multiplayer levels in Quake have very different requirements than the multiplayer levels in the Battlefield series of games.

Going back to our Mario example, if the level design team didn't build spaces that would test a player's ability to make Mario perform all of his best moves to get through them, then the game really isn't complete. For example, if the move Wall Jump is in the game, but the player never has to use the move to finish a level (or at least use it to find all the level secrets) then the game's design isn't being fully expressed.

How to Progress as a Level Designer

Level design is one of the most straightforward disciplines that you can dig in to. Play your favorite games, and take notes as you play. Write down how a level makes you feel, and try to notice how it is accomplishing that effect. Remember: everything that goes into a video game is designed, so there is always a reason for every thing that you see in a level. Try to figure out what those reasons are. You can also learn a lot by doing the same exercise with movies and TV. Those guys are masters at creating mood and telling story through their environment, so learn as much as you can.

Level designers are at their most effective when they can handle both ends of the level-creation process. That means that they can create the pieces that make up the physical space of their level and then they can do the assembly and scripting to bring it to life in-game. So once you've dug into trying to understand how levels are composed, next master 3-D modeling and level scripting.

There are tons of great blogs and articles on level design, and I am developing a series of books and video classes teaching level design fundamentals, but nothing can take the place of doing the work for yourself—of building spaces and seeing how players react to them.

Audio Designer

Audio design is closely tied to gameplay design. The more ways you can provide feedback to a player during a game, the better, and audio is one of the most powerful types of feedback. Each time a weapon fires or a bad guy gets damaged, the player expects to see and hear the results of those actions. But they also need to hear the results of everything else they do, from opening a door or swinging (and missing) with a machete, to opening the Pause menu and clicking on a new save game slot. Great audio goes almost unnoticed; it doesn't overpower the user but it reinforces everything they do in an intuitive, elegant way. And, of course, some games are lucky enough to have musical soundtracks, or even voice-over dialogue. All of those things fall under the purview of the audio design team.

Audio design is extremely painstaking. Imagine a beautiful, realistic scene in a modern first-person shooter game. If you take one of the guns and fire it at targets made of wood, steel, concrete and glass, you (as the player) expect to hear the correct sounds as bullets bounce off of (or blast through) all of those materials. Now multiply that by the number of different kinds of guns in the game. Now add in vehicles, water, melee combat, and more—it can be a dizzying amount of data. The audio design team keeps track of those assets and makes sure that everything sounds correct.

How to Progress as an Audio Designer

First, you need to learn how to create and edit audio. Handling sound files is a huge part of the job, as is tweaking sounds to get just the right tone.

Next, learn as much as you can about how sound engines work in games. When do particular sounds get played? How does the game determine which sounds have precedence? Which sounds are the most important to the gameplay designers? And to the level designers?

Finally, you can dig into music. Play your favorite games and see how music works in them. Is the music on all the time? Does it stop and start? When? And can you figure out why?

> ***Hardy Says***: *A lot of composers would like to put their music in games. If you're one of them, knowing how to do audio design gives you a real head start in that area.*

Narrative Designer

The role of narrative designer is relatively new in game development. The narrative designer is responsible for overseeing all the ways that the game could potentially tell the story. For example, if the game has "mission briefings" then the narrative designer might write the text that appears in them so that they have a uniform tone and reveal important parts of the story. They might also write the voice-over lines for actors to speak in-game, or create the audio snippets of recordings that the player can find to put pieces of the backstory together.

How to Progress as a Narrative Designer

This is a tricky question. The position of narrative designer seems to exist mostly on big, high-profile games. Smaller development houses probably don't have the budget to support someone who is just focused on storytelling. And the exact process is still evolving. Even the smartest, most creative narrative designers that I had the chance to work with in my career were still trying to figure out reliable methods of controlling the story flow in their games.

If you're intrigued by the idea of narrative design, I recommend that you focus on your writing. If you can produce compelling dialogue, create interesting characters, or bang out immersive scenes, those skills will give you a great springboard toward writing for games.

I'll leave you with one final thought, courtesy of a master;

"The first draft of anything is sh‡t."

- Ernest Hemingway

Once Upon a Time - In Game Design

Early in my career, I was fortunate to work with a small company named Luxoflux developing a car combat game called Vigilante 8. Luxoflux had hit a rough patch. They were originally signed to make a console version of the coolest PC game ever made—Activision's Interstate '76. But sales of Interstate '76 really didn't catch fire when it was released (people didn't understand just how cool it was). Activision chose not to make a console version of the game but wanted to preserve their relationship with Luxoflux. The head of development decided that a natural alternative would be for the small studio to make an arena-based car combat game like the much beloved Twisted Metal series of games.

It might have seemed like a natural alternative to business wonks, but the team was pissed. They loved Interstate '76 and they definitely weren't fans of the vehicle arena combat genre. Activision's plan was to send a wide-eyed, enthusiastic young designer (me) to help Luxoflux discover the love of the car-combat genre.

I remember watching a demo of Luxoflux's game engine. It was hilariously funny because the physics of the cars' axles were all wrong. They acted like rubber bands, so that when a car went over a bump, the body of the car would sway down low and then it would spring up into the air like a cartoon. If you drove over jumps at the right angle the car would bounce off the side and then catapult across the ground, rolling over and over across the landscape. It was hilarious blooper footage, but it also got me to thinking— the earliest versions of Twisted Metal really didn't have physics at all. Their movement was all just faked as they zipped around on flat ground. If the Luxoflux engine could let cars bounce and roll, maybe we could build a combat model that took advantage of that.

Peter was the designer and chief creative officer of the (then) tiny Luxoflux studio. He and I had a long talk about how much I loved Twisted Metal, and the conversation came around to the physics in the Luxoflux engine. I enthusiastically described a "bump and tumble" combat experience that could be unlike anything in Twisted Metal, and Peter simply nodded and made a few notes on the whiteboard, and that's what he set about designing for Vigilante 8.

The game was a hit, the studio stayed afloat, and went on to make sequels, prosper, and make new games for Activision. Ultimately they got bought by the mega publisher, and after a few years Peter and the other co-founder, Adrian (arguably the best tools programmer I ever worked with), left to form their own independent small studio and remake Vigilante 8 for web play.

That is the great "cycle of life" for the most successful developers in the industry—growth from small start-up to large studio to a "liquidity event," where the company that you built gets bought for its value. Then, eventually back to start-up mode to try and do it all again.

❋ Roles in Programming

You can't make a video game without programming a computer at some point. Actually, these days that's not entirely true. So many powerful tools and useful technologies exist out in the world that you can make a game with very little programming expertise. So let me revise my previous statement: You can't make a good video game without programming a computer at some point.

Programmer

Programmers are the heart of software development. They have mastered the intricate languages that tell the machines what to do and (in many cases) wrestled with the mathematics necessary to describe interesting ideas in terms of number systems.

Hardy Says: I've seen debates where folks have insisted that, because of advanced tools and technologies, modern programmers don't need to study complex math. If you only want to be a low-level programmer, responsible for implementing someone else's solutions to problems but never developing your own, then I suppose you might be able to sneak by without studying advanced math. But when you find that the heights of power and money are out of your reach, don't come crying to me.

Game programming can be a wild and woolly business. You don't have to wear a suit and a tie, but working in the entertainment sector requires some unique characteristics from programmers.

Unique characteristic #1: The ability to collaborate. We discuss this elsewhere in this series, but it bears repeating: interactive media is a collaborative art form.

Unique characteristic #2: Speed. It matters a lot. I've heard it said that programmers can get better at writing code, but they never get faster. Game development is a constantly shifting landscape, and the technical requirements that you were working toward today might be different next week, never mind what they'll be two years from now when you actually ship the game. Programmers who are nimble enough to react to those changes and still produce results quickly can thrive. If you are a naturally slow coder, or you're uncomfortable dealing with a rapidly shifting environment, then game development may not be the career for you.

Unique characteristic #3: Broad technical aptitude. As a technical person, you may be the only person around who knows anything about things, like how to replace a busted fan in a PC, what components to buy if you're going to scratch build your own development towers, or how to open up ports on a firewall. You may need to know how to strip and recap an Ethernet cable or how to update the firmware on a console dev kit. Issues like these come up all the time, especially on small teams. When the artists and designers are running around crying, and the producers are freaking out because the technical sky is falling, you'll be the only one who can fix it. (And yes, that will happen. A lot.)

How to Progress as a Programmer

As an entry-level programmer, you'll be asked to handle simple stuff. Chances are you'll be doing tasks that are fairly mundane and that you can figure out how to do by carefully reading forum posts and/or watching instructional tutorials online. After you earn your stripes, you may be asked to work on higher-profile tasks.

Sometimes a programmer will display an aptitude for a particular type of work and get drawn into working in that area. A great example of this is tools. Really good tools development is one of the biggest advantages a development team can have, but most programmers seem to want to work on the glory jobs (rendering, artificial intelligence, and gameplay code). If you aspire to work on particular systems, then try to show that you're good in that area. But if you're a great tools programmer, please do everyone else on your team a favor and embrace it! At the highest levels, you may become a lead programmer, or even a technical director, where you will help determine a team's, or even a company's, overall approach to technical development.

I'm not part of the programmer tribe, so I'm sure there are a lot of insider secrets that I don't know, but I can offer tips that have strengthened (or sabotaged) the careers of the folks I've worked with. In short, they are the general principles that I've advised for every discipline: develop the skills to interact with the other disciplines and then focus on collaborating with them. Learn how fast you work, make accurate time estimates, and then meet them. Make learning new technology a priority and, finally, never over-promise and under-deliver.

Oh, and learn math.

Technical Artist / Technical Designer

I'm including these two jobs in the programming category because, in a way, they have more in common with programming than with their associated disciplines. As software development gets more complex, it has become incredibly useful for teams to have people with strong technical knowledge and a background in a more artistic discipline (art or design).

The technical artist and the technical designer are go-betweens. Their job is to help connect the programming team to the needs of artists and designers. So, for example, let's say the artists needed a particular feature added to their tools. The technical artist would be the one to help define that need for the programmers. Then he or she would work with the programming team to figure out exactly how the new feature would be added to the tools, making sure that it would work in the best possible way for the art team.

Another role that technical artists and designers fill is helping to prioritize technical tasks. For example, imagine that the level designers were running into a little-known but highly frustrating bug that was doubling or even tripling the time it took them to build levels for the game. The technical designer could make the programming team aware of the bug and help make fixing it a higher priority for them to fix. The technical designer could even work to help the test team track down the bug and document it.

Technical artists and technical designers are also a team's in-house experts. It can be incredibly helpful for a team to have a resident expert who can train people how to use particular tools or software, or who can help the team learn and use best practices.

It's important to understand that technical artists and technical designers are not individual contributors. That means that they probably won't ever make content that the audience will see. These jobs also tend to exist more on big teams, but I've seen start-ups grab talented folks in this field as founders just so they were on board from day one.

How to Progress as a Tech Designer / Artist

If you're a highly technical person but you still think of yourself as an artist or a designer, then you may already be on this career path. First, learn everything you can about the tools and technology that your team is using.

> **Hardy Says**: *That will take a while.*

Meanwhile, develop your skills as a teacher. Practice by giving individual or group classes on what you've learned, or by writing guides on software or best practices for your teammates to use. Next, branch out and study tools and technology from all over. Learning how different smart people solved similar problems can teach you a lot about what's possible, what works, and what doesn't.

❋ Roles in Art

Someone once explained to me the difference between fine art and commercial art, and it has helped me understand the role of artists in the workplace ever since. Put simply, fine art is art that you do to satisfy yourself. Nobody told Pablo Picasso that, "These cubist paintings aren't art. They make ladies look ugly." Nor did they tell Damien Hirst that, "A shark preserved in a glass box full of formaldehyde isn't art, it's just gross."

Actually, people might have said that stuff to those guys, but it didn't stop them from pursuing their own artistic visions and producing amazing pieces of art. fine art isn't made to sell or to make the artist famous. It's created to make a personal statement. Sure, it might be worth something when you're finished making it. It might even make you so famous that you become immortal in the annals of art history. But it might just sit in your mom's attic until one particularly aggressive spring cleaning when it all gets thrown away.

Commercial art is just the opposite. It is art created specifically to satisfy the needs of a client, and it's done to make the artist money. The "client" can be a lot of things. For example, if you're a concept artist working on a science fiction movie, then your client is probably the movie director. If all you can paint is really adorable cats, then they're going to replace you with another artist.

Video game art is commercial art. Artists on a development team have specific roles, and the art they produce must meet the needs of one or more clients.

Let's return to our concept artist example, only this time let's imagine they work in video game development instead of in the movies. Just like in the movies, a game concept artist needs to satisfy at least one client—their boss, probably the game's art director. But they also need to meet the requirements of the other disciplines on the team. For example, the concept artist might be asked to create a visual design for a bad guy and, for gameplay purposes, the gameplay designers need it to have a pointy head. In that case, the designers are clients as well. And with all game art, the programming team defines strict requirements for how the art should be built. If a game scene or character is too complex, then it can't be drawn correctly on-screen, so it's usually up to the technical team to set limits for everything that appears on-screen. In that way, the technical teams are "clients" on every piece of art that goes into the game. Finally, the game itself is the ultimate client. Imagine that our hypothetical artist was working on a Mario game. If the artist couldn't (or wouldn't) adopt the whimsical art style of the Mario franchise (sometimes called the brand) then they wouldn't be addressing the needs of the game.

Art Terms

Let's define some basic art terms so that things are clear as we move forward.

2-D, or **two-dimensional art**, is a catchall term that describes traditional forms of art such as paintings, drawings, graphic design, or typography. Some artists still use traditional tools such as brushes, paint, or pen and ink to create modern versions of 2-D art, but most modern 2-D art is created using digital tools like Adobe Photoshop or Adobe Illustrator.

3-D, or **three-dimensional art**, is a catchall term that describes art created using computer-aided design (CAD) software on computers. Instead of drawing 3-D art, modern artists use tools like Autodesk Maya or Pixologic ZBrush to model three-dimensional shapes that appear solid.

Animation is the art of making static images appear to move. Modern artists use both 2-D and 3-D techniques to create animations in video games.

The **user interface** (UI) is the series of menus and buttons that the player uses to control things outside the active part of the game, for example, things like the game select screen, the save game interface, and the options menu—these are all considered parts of the UI.

The **heads-up display** (HUD) keeps critical information on display for the player while the game is going on. It might include things like your score or how much health your character has left or even show you a map of the game around you.

We talked about the differences between fine art and commercial art and we defined some terms. Now let's dig into the jobs that artists do.

2-D Artist

Even on modern game development teams, a number of art jobs still require artists to have strong 2-D skills. If you're a fantastic 2-D artist but you don't know a thing about 3-D art, then you might find work doing jobs like these. But it's important to point out that many modern artists have both 2-D and 3-D skills, so pure 2-D art jobs are rare, and the caliber of people in those positions is extremely high. If you decide this is the career path for you, it can be a difficult road to follow.

Concept Artist

We've all seen examples of amazing concept art from games, movies, and TV. Just like objects in the real world, everything that appears in a movie, TV show, or game needs to be designed. Concept artists are the fantastically talented digital painters who take evocative descriptions of places, things, or characters and turn them into inspiring visuals.

Most concept artists are graduates of highly prestigious art schools, such as the Art Center College of Design or the Rhode Island School of Design, which have a well-deserved reputation for turning out the best of the best. Graduates from these programs are often hired right out of school to design things like cars and theme park rides, or to paint concept art for television and movies. Sometimes high-profile artists from other fields, like comic books, can end up doing concept artwork as well.

In many ways, the job of concept artist is the holy grail of art jobs. You are paid to simply imagine awesome stuff and produce pictures of it. Hopefully, this gives you some idea of the kind of work that the top concept artists in the business are capable of. Artists such as Craig Mullins and Alex Ross aren't just talented, they've spent years honing their craft to the point where they can quickly and efficiently produce amazingly refined images of whatever a client might want.

How to Progress as a 2-D Artist

Start by getting good foundational art training, which will probably be focused on mastering some style of traditional 2-D art. Be sure to delve into digital painting as you progress. You can do some types of concept design work in traditional 2-D mediums, but nothing can replace the power and flexibility of working in a digital format.

As you progress through your training, you will undoubtedly see opportunities to practice your skills for various clients along the way. Jump at those chances, even if they're unpaid. Stay humble, and seek out the pros. Show them what you've got, and ask for their guidance. Then, listen carefully to their advice.

It's a hard climb to get to where you want to be. Stick to it and don't give up, but always be honest about your own talent level.

Graphic Designer

Modern life is filled with examples of graphic design—from movie posters and car logos to the arrangement of letters on the package of a loaf of bread—all the work of skilled artists.

Graphic design is a serious field, and the best examples of it stand the test of time by building a brand and an identity that are indelible in the minds of their customers. Graphic design for games occurs in two main areas: the user interface (UI) and the heads-up display (HUD). These are areas of game development where real innovation can lead to huge wins for a development team. The competitive landscape of game development is littered with games that did a poor job on their interface, while the games that did it best sell kajillions of copies and are hailed as works of genius.

There are challenges to working as a graphic designer. First, it's a crowded field. Everything needs to be designed, and a lot of folks would like to do this job. Modern schools churn out countless degrees and certificates in things like graphic design, web design, and communications arts, so it can be hard to stand out in the crowd.

Add to that the very real fact that graphic designers are the most overlooked professional category in game development (yes, even more than audio designers). Development teams always put off interface design until late in the development process, and not always because of bad planning. Often the delay comes from the fact that a team doesn't quite know what game they're making, so finalizing the interface can be difficult.

3-D Artist

3-D artists use CAD programs to create three-dimensional models of objects that appear in games or movies. 3-D art is used everywhere from TV commercials to corporate logos. Even shows that look like they are 2-D (like the Simpsons) are constructed out of 3-D models and then animated to look flat. It's cheaper and more consistent to make content that way rather than drawing the same stuff by hand over and over.

If this career path interests you, one important factor to be aware of is that the technical bar for 3-D art is getting higher and higher. Top-tier artists need to be technically adept to produce spectacular results, and the field is getting more complex all the time. If you want to reach the top, be prepared to embrace the technology as well as the beauty.

There are two broad categories of 3-D artist: those who specialize in environment art and those who specialize in characters. Both jobs are similar, for example, they both use many of the same CAD tools to create models, and the techniques for building and decorating (texturing) those models are the same.

But as you'll see, the two jobs have very different goals.

3-D Character Modeler

The goal of the character modeler is to make every digital actor that appears on-screen a unique work of art. Sometimes the objective is to try and make the characters realistic, sometimes not. But a successful 3-D character is always engaging and memorable.

How to Progress as a 3-D Character Artist

Just like other art jobs we've discussed, the best grounding for either path is solid traditional art training. Once you're on your way studying the fundamentals of art, you'll need to become intimately familiar with CAD modeling software. There are a few types, but by far the most prevalent are Maya and ZBrush.

I recommend that you study successful character designs you see in popular media. Start by studying the character designs in TV shows, movies, anime—whatever you like best. But make sure to branch out from the stuff you're most familiar with and broaden your sensibilities. No commercial artist spends the entirety of their career making only their favorite characters.

> ***Hardy Says****: Many of the best 3D Character Modelers enjoy the art form so much that they make a lot of 3D art in their spare time. It's not at all uncommon to find their portfolios filled with original characters and scenes, as well as unique takes on popular characters and creatures. It's a great way to build up your portfolio and strengthen your skills.*

3-D Environment Modeler

The goal of the 3-D environment artist is to make settings that are evocative, immersive and most importantly convincing. Sometimes their settings need to be realistic, while other times they may be pure fantasy.

Instead of making each piece of a scene memorable, their goal is to make each "digital movie set" a beautiful composite of elements that work together by using architectural techniques like composition, staging, lighting and more. And often the environment needs to be subtle enough to frame the action of the characters without overshadowing them.

How to Progress as a World Modeler

Environment artists focus on the level design in games. Play your favorite titles from the beginning and, as you play, study what the environment artists included in their work and try to figure out why.

As you immerse yourself in successful level designs, learn a little about architecture, a little about landscaping, and a little about lighting. You don't need to be Frank Lloyd Wright, but there's a wealth of knowledge and technique out in the world so that you don't have to try and reinvent on your own.

Finally, build some environments. Make some simply for show, but also try your hand at creating stuff to put into a game. To build up your skills and your portfolio, practice by making assets for a game or mod that you love to play.

Animator

Animators make things move on the screen. Sometimes they work in 3-D, moving characters and props. Other times they work in 2-D animating buttons, flashes, text, special effects, and anything else that needs to look like it has a life of its own on-screen.

3-D animation has two important steps. First, 3-D character models must be rigged for 3-D animation. 3-D animations don't just grab the model and move it around. Instead, the animator must "rig" the model with a series of digital "bones" that are connected to every part of the model. These bones are the pieces that the animators actually animate, causing the attached body parts to move and making the character move on-screen. Rigging a model can be a painstaking process, especially if the thing that's going to be animated has complex pieces like hair, fur, or cloth.

Once a model is rigged, the animators can build animations for it. Occasionally, senior animators will create the key frames of an animation (the main poses that the model should pass through) and then have junior artists clean up the frames in between so the entire action looks smooth. Another common approach to dividing up the work is to put the "signature animations" in the hands of more senior artists, while the junior team members handle more mundane tasks, like character walk cycles.

Motion Capture

Motion capture is another animation technique common in video games and movies. In the motion-capture technique, instead of an animator hand-animating the key frames of actors and props, special cameras record the movements of objects in the real world and translate those movements into animation data on the screen.

Recording motion-capture data requires special studios equipped with multiple digital cameras surrounding the performance area. Motion-capture performers need adequate room to perform the required actions, so depending on what kind of data is being captured, motion-capture studios can be quite large.

Anything that's going to be recorded has to have special markers attached so that the digital cameras capture every nuance of movement and turn them into computer data. Motion-capture performers wear special suits with the markers attached, or even have markers glued to their skin and then perform their movements normally. Motion-capture data is particularly good for animations that have a distinctive look in the real world. For example, the movements of athletes, especially big-name stars at the top of their respective sports.

How to Progress as an Animator

As with the other types of art jobs, a good foundation in art is a great place to start. Of course, your training should transition as soon as possible to actual animation. You don't need to know all that jazz about character design or about how to build a convincing 3-D environment: you need to make characters move on-screen!

To improve, study the masters. Start with traditional 2-D classics and work your way up to modern 3-D animated sequences that you admire. How are the characters framed? What are the key poses in the animation? Why? How do the artists show weight? Momentum? Emotion?

> ***Hardy Says***: *Talented animators are a little bit like airplane pilots; they can't keep themselves away from the thing that they love. Have you already dabbled in making animations? There is a need for talented animators. If you are one, then embrace it.*

❈ Make Your Own Break

Ok, you've done your prep work, you've learned some skills, and you've finished some projects. That's a good start. Now, to land a job in the game development industry, you're going to need to follow the principle of extreme persistence.

Let's go get a job!

Anyone can develop technical skills; all it takes is hard work and perseverance. But if you have the right stuff to be working in professional game development, you will find, or manufacture, your own break.

Once Upon a Time - In Extreme Persistence

I once encountered an aspiring level designer named Chris who embodied extreme persistence perfectly. Chris was studying at a university with a declared major in "virtual space design." It wasn't a real thing at the time, but he was fascinated by video game levels and so he'd talked his professors into letting him study them as a major.

Chris happened to see a seminar given by one of my coworkers at a professional conference. Afterwards, he approached my coworker and politely asked if he could have a business card. He waited for a couple of days and then sent a follow-up e-mail, thanking the coworker and asking a few questions about game development. My coworker, flattered, was only too happy to answer them. But every time he answered, Chris sent more questions. And they got more and more technical until my coworker showed up at my desk, exasperated. "Hardy, this guy keeps sending me e-mails, asking questions about level design. Please get rid of him."

I read the e-mail thread, and I looked over Chris's online portfolio. He had some interesting ideas, but he had clearly never tried out his ideas on actual users. I responded to Chris's last e-mail, thanking him for his interest. I said that while some of his designs looked promising, he had a lot more to learn about the practical side of designing virtual spaces.

Chris immediately replied and thanked me for looking at his stuff and asked another question: "What kinds of things should I be learning?"

I had to admire his determination. He wasn't going to be put off by a simple, polite response, so we exchanged a few e-mails as I took over the thread, giving him tips and pointers. But things got super-busy on the project I was working on, and I just didn't have time for mentoring anyone in level design, so I let the thread drop.

A month later, I was sitting at my desk with my headphones on when a stranger appeared and waved to get my attention. This was unusual, because I was working at a big company and the studio space was behind doors locked by magnetic security cards. I tugged off my headphones, and the guy smiled sheepishly.

"Hi my name is Mike. I'm sorry to bother you, but I'm a friend of Chris. I work in a different division of the company, but he asked me to come down to your offices and see if my key card could open your studio doors."

I was stunned. "What can I do for you Mike?"

He dragged a spare chair over and sat down next to me and then pulled out a notepad and pen.

"Chris knows that you're too busy to answer his e-mail. So he asked me to come down here on my lunch break and just take a few notes for him on the last round of questions that he sent you."

I had to laugh. Chris was absolutely not going to be denied! I pulled up the last e-mail and answered the questions verbally as Mike took detailed notes. Then he thanked me and left with an awkward wave.

One month later, my producer and I determined that we needed one more contract artist to finish the work that we were doing, and Chris immediately sprang to mind. I decided that his persistence had earned him a shot. We hired him, and Chris has been working in the industry ever since.

Making a List

Be organized about your job search. Take the process of looking for a job as seriously as you would doing a job at the company you'd like to work for. Make a list of the places you're applying to and take notes on your steps. For example, keep a record of when you first apply, and what response you got. Keep track of notes, if the company gets in touch and talks to you, and capture any assignments that they give you as well.

Being organized about your search helps you in three big ways. First, it helps you look professional in the eyes of potential employers. If you're on top of the process and buttoned up about what's going on, it can greatly help your interactions with the company.

Second, it's critical to remember what jobs you're actually pursing. If you find twenty jobs online and apply for all of them, it's not only possible but very likely that you'll forget about some of them (I have). You might miss key communications, or fail to follow up when you should.

The third bit of practical advice is something nobody seems to mention. If you're out of work and looking for a job, and you apply for unemployment benefits, you can only collect your unemployment insurance checks if you continually prove to the government that you're looking for work. That means that at any time you might be called on to produce proof that you've been talking to various companies and trying to find a job. If you're all caught up on your "I want to get hired" files, that process is a snap. If not, then Uncle Sam might come looking to get their unemployment insurance money back.

Résumé and Portfolio

It's virtually impossible to just walk in the door and get a job interview based on your résumé. One of the reasons that I stress practical experience so much is because it is proof that you can do the work. A portfolio of examples speaks volumes about you as a potential employee. Companies can view your examples and quickly judge if you're the kind of person they'd like to hire. If all they have to look at is a résumé or CV, then you're already several steps behind better prepared candidates.

Two important things about your résumé and cover letter: first, make it incredibly easy to read. If a hiring manager has to dig through huge blocks of text spread out across eight pages just to find relevant experience or keywords, then you're doing it all wrong. Second, make it stand out in a crowd. How you do that is up to you.

General Tips

- Bring multiple copies of your cover letter and current résumé with you.

- Have prints of your artwork in your portfolio and have digital versions available. It can also be incredibly helpful to have your portfolio online so that interested managers can simply pull up your work and take a look at it.

- For gameplay design or level design, having a playable copy of your game available can work wonders. If not, a video capture of the gameplay is great.

- For level or character art, stills are great because they show what your environment looks like when it's all assembled. But also be sure to show the pieces separately, and show un-textured models as well as associated texture maps.

- Animators will need a "reel," with examples of their work. I recommend showing as many types of animation as you can, including character action, rigid body, and squash and stretch.

> **Hardy Says:** *Smart hiring managers will have played the stuff you worked on. Be prepared to talk about it intelligently.*

If your résumé lists previous work experience, hiring companies are allowed to check with those employers to confirm that you actually worked there during the time period and in the job that you specified. Generally, the company you previously worked for won't say anything about your job performance or the circumstances around your leaving. That's because if they said anything that kept you from getting a job, you could conceivably sue them for damaging your career. So if you had an emotional breakdown on the sales floor of Hot Topic, quit, and stormed out never to return, it's not a problem. If the hiring company checks your references, Hot Topic will simply report how long you were a part of their team and your end date. But if your breakdown got out of hand and led to an arrest and criminal charges, then the hiring company will probably find out about that, which is a whole different story.

(Anti) Social Media

Social media and the connectedness of the information age have made it easy for companies to find out a lot about potential employees. And they do. Companies that are interested in hiring you will check any references that you provide, and they will often check your credit scores. If you have a presence on social media, they will find it and look at it. So if you're lucky enough to get an interview, make sure there's nothing present in social media (or elsewhere) that might sabotage your chances of landing a job.

__Hardy Says__: True story - I once received a résumé from a woman that included links to her online modeling portfolio. Unfortunately, her portfolio also included shots from a Playboy photoshoot that she'd done. They were tasteful, but still 100% nude. She had a lot to offer a potential employer <ahem>, but seeing her in that context made hiring her out of the question.

Job Hunting: About Eggs and Baskets

When you're searching for a job, keep an open mind during the process. Don't keep all of your eggs in one basket, that is, don't just follow one lead, hoping it will be the opportunity you want. Be smart: even though jobs can be tough to come by, the right candidate is a valuable thing to find. The more tied down you are to particular things, the harder it can be to find a position. For example, if you really want to live in a specific city or part of the country, then the pool of jobs that you can apply for gets smaller.

__Hardy Says__: When I got my break into game development I moved from New York City straight to Los Angeles. That was a big shift in culture, but that willingness to follow the work helped me find some terrific opportunities and had a positive impact on my career.

I also recommend being flexible about particular companies, or even job titles. People like to ask me about the best team I ever worked on, and I always say the same thing, "Every team I was ever on was the most talented team I ever worked with."

I'm not being glib—it's true. Every team has unique strengths that can be leveraged to make a terrific product. Even small teams with very little experience can produce miraculous results if they have a strong culture and teammates who are committed to a shared project vision. Great work is going on all over the place—on large teams and small, at established companies and start-ups. Don't limit yourself. Be open, and then do your part to help make whatever team you end up on into a dream team.

When job searching, watch out for jobs that pop up repeatedly but never seem to get filled or stay filled. Those are evidence of organizational problems.

Once Upon a Time - In Job Hunting

There is a high-profile game development studio that's been in business for a long time, and roughly once every year or so I notice them looking for a senior gameplay designer. I tracked down someone who had previously filled the role and managed to get a personal account from them about the studio. The reason the job kept appearing was twofold. First, the studio was located in the middle of Nowhere, California. The town was lovely, but employees that worked there, and their families, began to feel isolated and cut off from the outside world. Second, the studio leadership had come out of the television and movie industry. One was a powerful executive producer with a wall full of Emmys, and the other was a long-haired creative guru who favored rock-n-roll leather pants. The pair were dynamic and smart, but neither of them knew much about making games, so the senior gameplay design role was created to bring in someone with game development experience to make a game based on whatever the executives said. While the high profile of the studio made the position attractive, the isolation and the lack of creative authority in the role quickly burned candidates out.

Interviewing

Game development is a collaborative art form. The exact mixture of personalities and temperaments in a game studio are what make it unique and give it its character, so most hiring companies use a process called a HIRE/NO HIRE loop when somebody comes in to interview. Generally, the people who participate in an interview loop are those you'd be working with the most. Some might be your managers; others might be working alongside you. Sometimes companies even give employees the chance to interview potential managers who would be managing them.

Candidates will generally be asked to speak to a succession of people. Each interviewer is included in a special e-mail that goes out when the candidate is present in the studio. The e-mail usually says <Name of Person> <Job They Want> HIRE/NO HIRE in the e-mail header. Each time a person interviews the candidate, they rush back to their office to whip out an e-mail with their recommendation in it—either HIRE or NO HIRE. As the day winds on, interviewers update the e-mail thread with their notes. Folks will offer their thoughts about what went well, or badly, and may occasionally offer specific topics for later interviewers to drill down on. For example, if a candidate happened to mention that they had a deathly fear of computer keyboards, later interviewers might follow up with more questions about that. Generally, the last person you speak to is the person who actually has the power to hire you or not, so if they're not convinced, it's not going to happen.

If you get all HIRES, you're in. The people who spoke to you all thought you'd be a great fit for the culture and that you had the right stuff. Since that's pretty self-explanatory, let's focus on NO HIRE.

Even one NO HIRE vote is a big red flag. A NO HIRE vote means that one of those folks doesn't think you'd be a good fit. However, it doesn't always mean that you won't get the job. Sometimes it just means that one interview didn't go well. That's why there's a loop. If you feel like one conversation didn't go as well as you were hoping—don't despair. It can still turn out all right. Try to shake it off and fix whatever went wrong in the next conversation.

General Tips

- If you want the job, act like you want to be there.

- Most game development companies follow a casual dress code. Dress casually, but nice.

- Make sure you're well groomed before you go. Shower. Wash your hair. Wear deodorant. Make sure your clothes and shoes are clean.

- If you express your wild sense of individuality through extreme hair styles or fashion, I suggest that you dial it back. If that sounds harsh, sorry; development teams have to work in close proximity to each other for long hours at a time.

- Avoid disgusting bodily habits. Don't fart in an interview. Don't pick your nose. Don't chew your nails or pick scabs. If you're offered lunch, use your manners and chew with your mouth closed.

- Avoid swearing during an interview.

- Avoid revealing clothes, or baring what is generally considered private skin.

- Be honest. I've actually had someone submit a résumé for a position where they claimed to have worked on a small project that I led. I'd never met the person, or even heard their name before. Needless to say, they didn't get the job. But beyond that, I let people in my network know that the person was claiming work experience that they really didn't have, and to be careful if they were considering that person for a job.

- Finally, I also recommend not saying things that you think the interviewers want to hear, or trying to talk about stuff that you don't really understand. If you're worried about your lack of experience with a particular subject, just be honest and don't try to fake it.

Once Upon a Time - In Interviewing

I was walking to lunch with a candidate applying for an art director position at a very large company. On the way to the restaurant, someone in our group quipped, "So you're an art director huh? Do you sit around and play with your color wheel all day?"

The candidate brusquely replied, "Oh, I don't believe in color theory. I'm a digital artist."

I realized immediately that this person did not have a real, fundamental knowledge of art. He had managed to bluff his way through the interviews up to that point, but he had no business in an art director position for a major game franchise. I quietly had a word with the executive producer and the company sent him on his way.

If the candidate had simply come clean and admitted that he didn't have a strong understanding of traditional color theory, he still wouldn't have gotten the job, but the outcome in this case was worse; the company came to the conclusion that he was a phony, and couldn't trust a word he said.

You Shall Be Tested

Many teams will ask aspiring developers to take some kind of a test during the hiring process.

Tests can help the hiring team gauge a number of things about an applicant like their general skill level, how well they take direction, how quickly they can accomplish tasks and the quality of the final work (aesthetically, technically etc.). If you're asked to take a test, I have two recommendations for you.

First, accept the test with enthusiasm: I've met a number of candidates who were reluctant to do any kind of work in the hiring process. Sometimes their hesitation came from fear that the team was somehow going to "steal their work." Other times, the candidate felt like they were "working for free," and that the team was going to somehow take what they'd done and use it in a product. Here's my answer: nobody does that. Nobody. I've never been on a development team that had too few creative ideas. The notion that a team might somehow need to steal your great idea and run off to make a zillion dollars with it is absurd.

I've heard it said that ideas are cheap, but I disagree with that statement. Great ideas are valuable. Incredibly valuable. Maybe even invaluable, because if you don't have an inspiring, exciting idea that gets people fired up and working, you've got nothing at all. But big ideas are extensions of the soul of the artist that created them. We see examples of this all the time in popular culture; movie directors who continually make terrific movies in a particular franchise, but then when a new director steps in the following movies are terrible. That's because the creative sensibilities of the artist infuse the final work. Every choice made along the way is shaped by the people who are actually making the choices. Different people mean different decisions. And there's no way to count the number of big and small decisions that equal a finished project in any discipline.

Hardy Says*: A fellow named Jason, one of the original founders of Bungie, is the driving creative force behind that studio. He's a legitimate creative genius, and everyone who has ever worked on a Bungie game knows that his unique insight and his spark of creativity are part of what make their products special. Toward the end of working on the first Halo game, there were still hundreds of questions to be answered about critical elements. Subsequently, at times a line of people were waiting outside Jason's cubicle to review critical decisions with him to make sure the choices reflected his sensibilities. The takeaway? The only way to "steal" Jason's ideas would be to actually take Jason himself. (And no, I'm not endorsing that action)*

Second, over-deliver on whatever they're asking for: If the team is asking for a little bit of work, do more. Or else do the work in a surprising way, so that they can't help but be impressed. But remember to do your best quality work. The key is to figure out a way to over-deliver in a way that plays to your strengths. If they ask you to make one thing, and your first instinct is to make three things, but three would only be one-third as good as one thing done well, then that's not the right approach to over-delivering.

Once Upon a Time - In Over-Delivering

When I got my break into the industry, I was communicating remotely with a game director who was overseeing a high-profile project starring the first Hollywood A-list actor to participate in a video game—Bruce Willis.

The director had been tasked with creating a new intellectual property from scratch for the game. That's a big job, especially when there's a Hollywood star attached. The development team had already done some brainstorming for the game setting, but the director wanted to put more creative muscle behind the effort and was looking for creative help.

He asked me for two ideas for settings that would make for cool games. Instead, I sent him a list of ten concepts, all written out with enough definition so that what was cool about them was immediately evident. That won me the freelance writing job, and he gave me the briefing for the actual work.

The director had two weeks to prep for a meeting with Bruce Willis to pitch the story for the game. My job was to provide enough material to sell Willis on the creative side of the work. The team had kicked around some loose ideas about a setting featuring the Four Horsemen of the Apocalypse, but the director needed that concept to be fully defined. He also wanted a backup idea just in case the horsemen thing didn't fly. I asked him if there were any particular movies or influences that he wanted to include. It turned out that there had been a Planet of the Apes movie marathon on cable TV, and he'd binge-watched the entire thing, so my mission was to do something cool with the Four Horsemen of the Apocalypse and come up with something new based on Planet of the Apes. But instead of apes, I should use robots.

By the time I had finished developing the backstories and supporting sketches, the director had plenty of material to take to his meeting. I asked if I could come, but apparently it was an intimate affair. The "convo" went down at Bruce's pad, and his agent was there (so Hollywood). The result? Bruce felt that the stuff I'd developed for the Four Horsemen concept would work fine for a game, but he was particularly impressed by the "Planet of the Robots" concept. He thought it might make a good movie, and he asked who wrote it. The game publisher made me a job offer the very next day.

So to recap—if they ask you to take a test, do it enthusiastically and then make sure to knock their socks off by playing to your strengths and doing what you do best.

Follow Up

I used to always hear about how important it was to follow up on an interview. Most recruiter types say that it's appropriate to follow up with a nice "thank you" e-mail the day after the interview. I agree with that advice, but not just because it's nice.

In my experience, most companies know within a day or two if they want to hire you. But sometimes the interviews went well, but the hiring manager just didn't pull the trigger on the deal. This can happen for a lot of reasons, but the most common one is that there are several candidates lined up to interview and your interview just happened to fall at the front of the pack. Unfortunately, in cases like this, "out of sight is out of mind."

As additional candidates come through the door for the job, strong potential hires that came before can start to seem a little stale. The way to address this is through your follow-up e-mail.

Before you leave any interview, be sure to ask when the company will get back to you about the position, and how they prefer to get in touch. E-mail? Phone call? Both?

In your follow-up e-mail the next day (not the same day—you don't want to seem too eager) thank them and say how excited you are about the opportunity. If you left the interview with a good feeling, then it could also be an opportunity for you to include one or two questions that you didn't think to ask face to face. This is also your chance to inquire (in the nicest possible way) how the process of hiring is going.

Send the second follow-up one week later. Repeat that you're excited about the opportunity and then find an artful way to mention one thing about your interviews that will help them remember you. Then politely ask when you might expect an answer on the position. For example:

Dear <hiring manager>,

I wanted to say again how much I enjoyed meeting you and your team. <Your project> looks terrific, and I'm excited about the possibility of joining your team.

By the way, I was playing <some other game> the other day, and I came across a game mechanic that was similar to the one we were discussing. It was a fun way to implement that solution. I hope you get a chance to check it out.

I look forward to hearing from you about the position at your earliest convenience.

Best,

<Your name here>

Two follow-up notes. No more. Be polite and brief. After all, you should have more irons in the fire.

❋ Landing the Job

Let's say that you received a job offer. Congratulations! Great work on your preparation and your interview. The company wants you. It's important to remember that as we move on to the steps between a successful interview, being offered the job of your dreams, and your first day at the job. Let's take a look at them, just to cover our bases.

A job offer is the first step in a negotiation with a potential employer. I'm not going to tell you to play hardball, especially if you're just launching your career. But it's important to remember that once you accept a job, you'll be living with whatever kind of compensation you agreed to at the start. I remember when I landed my first job in the industry. The salary sounded like more money than I could even imagine and I gratefully accepted the offer right away. But there are some things that I wish I had known before I signed on the dotted line. Here are some things to check into:

- Get paid an amount of money that you can live with. Check a cost-of-living calculator for the area where the company is located. That will help you understand what your standard of living will be like with the money that you're being offered.

- Does the company offer a relocation plan? If you have to move to take the job, will the company pay for your relocation or do you have to pay for it out of your own pocket? Sometimes companies will offer a sum for relocation, and it's up to the employee to spend that money however they choose. So, for example, you might hire a moving company to move you, or you might try to put a lot of stuff into a rental truck and move yourself and save some dough—your choice.

- Are there other parts of the compensation package besides money?

- What are the company's benefits? How many vacation days does the company offer? How many paid sick days? Does the company offer any kind of insurance (health insurance or life insurance)? Do they have a policy on helping employees with a retirement plan?

· Does the company offer any sort of incentive-based compensation? This is a very important question. Things like stock incentives, stock options, or performance-based bonuses are how you will earn real money on the job. Yes, working happily at your job for years, saving money, and keeping yourself "in the black" budget-wise will help you get ahead. But if you aspire to make big jumps in your standard of living, these kinds of compensation are where that will happen.

> **Hardy Says**: Don't get too excited about the promise of discretionary bonuses. When Bungie shipped the first Halo game, one of the 3D artists sent an e-mail to the head of Microsoft complaining about the surprisingly small bonus checks for that project. The team figured that shipping such a monumental game would significantly raise their standard of living. After all, Halo was fairly popular...

But nope. Microsoft senior management sent an e-mail back to the entire studio saying, "You got bonuses. Be grateful." The continuing battle between Bungie and Microsoft about compensation on the Halo franchise was one of the key things that drove the studio to pull away from Microsoft and reclaim their status as an independent studio.

Once Upon a Time - In Contract Land

At one point in my career, I was laid off from my job in Los Angeles and scrambling to find a new position. I had three leads that I was pursuing at the time: one was with a company in Las Vegas, one was at a company that would have been closer to my family on the East Coast, and one was at a big-name console company in San Jose.

I had an "in" at the Vegas studio—a producer that I'd worked with knew me and was recruiting me heavily to go there and help them out. I'd found out about the job in San Jose through a friend who worked there. But I'd sent my résumé to the East Coast job cold, hoping that my experience might help me get a foot in the door.

Eventually, I got a call from the producer in Vegas with a job offer. It was not particularly generous, but I hadn't heard anything back from any of the other jobs and I was getting desperate.

Finally, the Vegas producer called me and asked if I was going to accept their offer. I was honest with him. I told him that I was excited about the project, but that I was hopeful about the job back East. Since we were friends, I asked him to be patient until I knew if the East Coast lead would pan out or not. He said, "Sure, don't worry about it. We'll talk soon."

Later that afternoon I got an e-mail from the executive producer at the Vegas company, saying that their job offer was only open for 48 hours. If they didn't hear back from me by the end of the following day, the offer would be considered closed and they would consider other candidates. I was welcome to reapply for the position but there was no guarantee that I'd be accepted.

Needless to say, that was devastating. The idea of moving to Vegas and working for low pay wasn't all that appealing, not to mention the fact that my acquaintance had used my own honesty against me. I wrestled with the choice all night, and finally at noon the next day I called the producer and said, "You want me, you got me. I'm on board."

It was a Friday, and he indicated that the company would be sending over the employment contract on Monday. I was relieved to have a job, but I hated the tactics they'd used.

Later that afternoon, I got a phone call from the executive producer at the San Jose company. I hadn't heard anything from them for weeks, so I had assumed that it wasn't going to work out, but to my surprise, he offered me a job. I had to be honest, so I said, "I'm sorry sir, but I've already accepted an offer from the company in Las Vegas." There was a pause on the line, and then he asked me, "What's the pay?"

Normally, I would never discuss compensation issues with a total stranger, but he insisted, so I told him. He made a sound that was a cross between a grunt and a snort. "Have you signed anything yet?" I explained that the papers would be sent on Monday and he cut me short. "I'll pay you double what they're offering, and I'll courier you the paperwork today." I giddily accepted and that was that, except for the dreaded phone call back to the producer in Vegas. Man, was he pissed at me. He started screaming at me, and I told him that he could stay mad about me accepting a better offer if I could stay mad about the strong-arm tactics that they had used to try and force me to sign on to their project. Then I hung up.

The producer from Vegas found me years later at a game industry trade show. He apologized for the strong-arm tactics and explained that the project had been in trouble for a long time. Senior management had been pressuring him heavily to fill the job fast. We shook hands and parted as friends.

That's business in the white-collar world. You're your own advocate and agent. You need to champion yourself, and don't be afraid to fight for things that you need.

It Ain't Personal

Getting a job in a creative industry can be like catching lightning in a bottle. I would offer this advice: don't take the process personally. As an aspiring developer on the outside looking in, you're only seeing a tiny part of the entire process. For example, when recruiters post jobs on public websites, the company may already have a particular person in mind for the job. But companies have to follow state and federal rules about posting jobs, so they follow through and advertise them even though they have no intention of bringing somebody new on board.

There's also an issue of timing. Companies have some strange quirks about how quickly (or slowly) things get done. Sometimes companies can shuffle along for years without taking action on important issues, but in other cases they can move with shocking quickness. Finding the right job, and in a time window when a company is prepared to commit to hiring someone, can be a challenge. Like so many things in life, there are people who will tell you no. They'll turn you away, or worse, simply overlook you entirely in favor of somebody else. As hard as it is, you can't let that deter you from moving on and trying again.

> **Hardy Says**: *The games industry can be a lot like riding a roller coaster, and at one point I was pretty close to rock bottom. I'd lost a job and failed to find a new gig for an achingly long time when a dear friend of mine told me the story of Colonel Sanders and his idea for Kentucky Fried Chicken.*
>
> *The Colonel (was that an actual military rank?) went on the road for years, and pitched his idea for KFC franchises hundreds of times before he finally found one person who bought into the idea. She called what Sanders had "extreme persistence," and that became a watchword for me. When I start to lose my fighting spirit, I remember the Colonel's extreme persistence, and it gives me hope and strength. And of course, fried chicken.*

❋ The Path to Leadership

Let's cut to the chase, shall we? A lot of aspiring game professionals have a vision for a game they'd like to make, and they want to know how to put themselves in the position to make that happen.

If you burn with the desire to make "your game," here's my advice: take it slow. You're not the only one with the desire to make your vision a reality. To accomplish your goal, you will need to mature in a number of important ways.

Do the following six things in your career, and I promise you'll get your shot:

1 Learn a skill, and then master it. Become an acknowledged expert on the matter for your team or company

2 Learn how to effectively communicate and collaborate with others

3 Become part of a team

4 Inspire the people around you through your work and your attitude

5 See a project all the way through, from conception to ship

6 Never start believing your own press

I can assure you, these steps will serve you well no matter what field you end up working in.

Afterword

Thanks for joining me for this walk through game development. I hope you've learned a lot and perhaps laughed a little.

If you enjoyed this book, or found it useful I'd be very grateful if you'd post a short review on Amazon, Goodreads, or on your favorite book-selling site. I personally read all your reviews, and use the feedback to make my books even better.

Thank you again for your support.

- Hardy LeBel

Made in the USA
San Bernardino, CA
28 February 2017